DESIGNOLOGY

How to Find Your PlaceType & Align Your Life With Design

DESIGNOLOGY

How to Find Your PlaceType
& Align Your Life With Design

Dr. Sally Augustin

Founder, Design with Science

CORAL GABLES

Published by Mango Publishing Group, a division of Mango Media Inc.

Cover and Layout Design: Elina Diaz

For permission requests, please contact the publisher at:
Mango Publishing Group
2850 Douglas Road, 2nd Floor
Coral Gables, FL 33134 USA
info@mango.bz

For special orders, quantity sales, course adoptions and corporate sales, please email the publisher at sales@mango.bz. For trade and wholesale sales, please contact Ingram Publisher Services at customer.service@ingramcontent.com or +1.800.509.4887.

This text benefitted from discussions the author had with Tamie Glass at the University of Texas at Austin and Lindsay T. Graham at the Center for the Built Environment, University of California at Berkeley.

Designology: How to Find Your Placetype and Align Your Life with Design

Library of Congress Cataloging
ISBN: (print) 978-1-63353-882-5 (ebook) 978-1-63353-883-2
Library of Congress Control Number: 2018962590
BISAC category code: HOM003000, HOUSE & HOME / Decorating

Printed in the United States of America

This text is dedicated to Denny Beasley (he knows the reasons why) and to Cristina Banks of the University of California, Berkeley, for all her support as this book was being developed.

Table of Contents

CHAPTER 1

WHAT IS ENVIRONMENTAL PSYCHOLOGY AND WHY DOES IT MATTER?

What Kind of Home and Workplace Are Best for You?

This can be a difficult question to answer.

Designing homes and workspaces is tough. Have you found yourself:

- Perplexed before a sea of paint chips at your local home improvement store?

- Wandering glumly through furniture stores?

- Endlessly cycling from one real estate showing to the next with an agent who is less and less concerned with finding you a home and more and more interested in getting you to buy something, anything, so the agent can move on to other clients?

- Decluttered and living in a string of desolate interiors?

- Opening your Pinterest account and just sighing?

The design-confused phase of your life is ending. You can take control of your physical world. The science-based information in the pages to come will show you how to create spaces where you and your family and friends can live your best lives.

With science, you can answer questions such as:

- What color should you paint your dining room?

- Should you use warm-colored light bulbs or cool ones in your office?

- How do shapes and patterns—on wallpapers, upholstery, or elsewhere—influence how you think in a space?

- How do room dimensions influence you psychologically? Can you use paint to make your living room feel like it's a more comfortable size or shape?

- In what ways do sounds affect your mental state? How should you soundscape places where you need to concentrate or think creative thoughts?

- Why does smell matter? How can you use scents to relax and feel less anxious? Remember things? Boost your mood?

- How do textures influence you emotionally? What should your bedroom rug feel like underfoot?

AND, perhaps the most important question of all:

- How are your personality and the best design approach for you really related?

You can use science-based design to develop interiors that align with your personality and support your real psychological needs—places where you feel comfortable, or creative, or whatever else you have planned. The pages that follow are packed with concrete, science-based design insights—in everyday language—that can be used to help you craft places where you can achieve your life goals.

What Is Environmental Psychology?

Place matters—and I didn't know how much it did until my standard of living depended on understanding the links between design, thoughts, and behaviors.

I was a grumpy client at the time of my enlightenment. I had been told by the executives who controlled my professional destiny to use all I'd learned in life and at school to develop retail spaces that encouraged sales, aligned with our brand…that basically ensured a prosperous and early-retired future for us all. But the thing was, I had no idea what to do. I didn't know which of the options that eager design teams were presenting I should OK.

So, I bluffed. Sometimes this worked much more successfully than other times—and sometimes not at all. These sometimes-not-at-all situations had the potential to have a negative effect on my earning power, so I resolved to cut out any design-related guesswork.

In my undergraduate days, I'd been exposed to enough science to think that there might be some sort of rigorously derived knowledge that could and should guide my decision-making. True to the training I'd received as a daughter of a librarian, I hunted for just such information until I found the science of environmental psychology.

Then I relaxed.

Environmental psychologists had investigated many of the issues that I needed to resolve, and applying their research findings made me look like a genius.

I was no longer a grumpy client.

To bolster my knowledge, I went back to school to study environmental psychology in a thorough, organized way. I now have lots of experience applying the science of environmental psychology in everyday settings.

My work as an environmental psychologist now takes me around the world, applying the science of environmental psychology and conducting studies myself. I use research-based insights to help organizations develop workplaces that boost professional performance and healthcare facilities whose aesthetics promote swifter healing. Retailers hire me to help create spaces that encourage sales, and academic organizations bring me in to inform the design of spaces where students learn best. Realtors have employed me to teach them how to stage homes that sell quickly for excellent prices. I work with individual homeowners to evolve current spaces or develop new ones, applying at their houses the same scientific principles that make such a difference in commercial, health care, academic, sales, and other environments.

You might call me a design shrink.

Environmental psychology is based in rigorous scientific research, not hunches. All the material in this book is drawn from carefully conducted studies, sometimes in laboratories, sometimes outside them. The way the research we'll cover was done means you can be confident using it to make design decisions.

As I discuss my own home redesign in the pages that follow, I'll be very briefly reviewing research findings that will be covered more thoroughly in the next chapters.

My House

Ten years ago, my husband and I bought a house for the value of the lot it stands on—the real estate equivalent of having the building thrown in for nothing. This really wasn't the bargain it might seem to be: homes that are pleasant places to live are not provided free of charge.

The reason most people give for buying a wreck is so they can create just the sort of home they want to live in. If you're ripping the walls down to the studs, you certainly aren't going to have to learn to live with many of the kitchen design choices previous owners have made—ditto for their living room wallpaper and master bathroom tile choices. We liked the idea of having a place tailored to our needs and desires and were also motivated to buy our house because it was inexpensive—in our part of the country, homes we want to live in cost more than we want to pay for them, if they're in good shape. The idea of eventually living in the sort of home we coveted was a motivator that keeps us scraping, grouting, and painting whenever we get tired of DIY-ing—which is often. We also both like the fact that we'd never seen a house before that looked like our home—it even came with a gargoyle already nestled in the brickwork at the roofline.

I am my own client when rehabbing my current home, but unlike doing surgery on yourself, being your own environmental psychologist can end well. Fixing up my own new home has shown me again how much more pleasant it is to live in a home that meshes with my personality and that applies research done by environmental psychologists. My significant other would agree, even though he's sometimes cranky because the most appropriate ways to refurbish a home are not necessarily the easiest and least expensive options.

The first crisis that confronted us in our new house was that many of its interior spaces were not daylit—ever.

Sunlight is a magical elixir.

Sunlight is a magic elixir for humans, and the home renovations and/or modifications that earn the biggest psychological returns on investment bring natural light into a space. I wanted the mood and cognitive performance boosts that numerous studies have linked to daylit interiors. I took down curtains and had interior walls eliminated to get natural light flowing throughout my home. I added windows and had heavy railings removed from one stairway because they blocked the flow of sunlight down that main staircase and into one end of our living room.

My husband was skeptical about my plans to move daylight through our home; they were expensive and disruptive, particularly during our winter construction marathon. (Note: if you live on the edge of the tundra, as we do, try not to end up without exterior walls in January.) My spouse is now an enthusiastic proponent of natural light. We currently have so much interior light that our next project is putting up minimalistic window blinds that will help keep down air-conditioning bills in the summer and eliminate occasional streaks of glare. One research project after another has found that human beings are better off physically and mentally when they sleep in a dark place, so we plan to add roll-up blackout blinds to sleeping areas.

Since seeing wood grain de-stresses people—which is consistent with our nearly universal quest for hardwood floors—my husband and I made sure that all of the unpainted wooden surfaces in our home, from floors to woodwork to cabinet fronts, were refinished. Convincing my husband this was a good idea was easy. Preserving unpainted wood, especially in woodwork, is much admired among the do-it-yourself crowd, and there are lots of products and services to help with this work. It also doesn't seem like it will be too difficult or time-consuming to refinish wood, at least until you start.

Since we live on a mini-size city lot, we have little access to soothing outdoor views, which makes the wood grain in our home even more important. We hope to add a water feature in our teeny backyard someday—research has shown that viewing water can be as restorative as seeing lush greenness. Right now, we get our outdoor fix on our roof deck; it's high enough off the ground to put us in the lush green treetops of our block.

Since your home is not only an echo of who you are now, but a tool you can use to become what you want to be in the future, we've made more changes to our home. Environmentally responsible living is important to us, and we want to become even more careful about using natural resources. We plan to add solar panels to our roof soon; when we rebuilt our decrepit garage, the floor was designed so that it could eventually link into a set of solar panels and store energy drawn from the sun. My husband and I each have havens in our home, and we set them up as soon as we could. My husband has a lab/workspace in our basement (full-size windows keep this area bright), and I have an office that opens up to a former sun porch. These spaces are sacred. I don't rearrange his; he doesn't set up camp in mine. We all need a space, a territory, where we can totally relax and make sense of the recent events in our lives. In previous, more open homes, we learned to respect the boundaries of each other's individual territories, even when no one could perceive them except us.

Just as people need privacy, they also need to socialize. We love the outdoors and entertaining there, but our small backyard makes a full-size deck at ground level impossible, so we head to the roof deck mentioned earlier with our friends. We have electrical outlets on our deck and can arrange the chairs there into a giant circle, because without eye contact, conversations suffer. We're shopping for a focal point for our rooftop retreat. When we add that focal point, it will be a place to which everyone's eyes can gracefully drift when conversations die down and we need to mentally regroup. It'll probably end up being a piece of all-weather art or an electric (no actual flame) fireplace. In the winter, we gather in our basement. It's where old comfortable couches and A/V equipment that only my husband really understands reside. I'm true to my PlaceType and love those couches, while my husband, also true to his PlaceType, prefers the rooftop single-person seats.

Seeing clutter really does make humans tense, so adding opaque built-ins to corral the clothes, papers, and odds and ends we've accumulated as we've lived life was a high priority. My husband built a window seat in our bedroom that has so much storage space that he doesn't need a separate dresser. We've made sure not to pack everything away—a stark, impersonal space would amp up our stress levels. A carefully curated set of tchotchkes populates every room in our home.

All the time we were adding windows and refinishing wood, I'd also been customizing the spaces in our home to support our personalities. I'm an Adventurer, and my husband's an Investigator (you'll learn more about PlaceTypes in coming chapters). We compromise on the design of our shared spaces, as described in Chapter 9. My husband is the cook, and the kitchen supports his PlaceType. Each of our PlaceTypes is fully expressed in our workspaces.

Molding our home to fit our psychological and physical needs, as well as keeping it from collapsing in a cloud of dust, will keep my husband and I busy for the foreseeable future. Each bit of progress we make inside and outside helps us restock our energy for DIY-ing—and makes my husband and me happier and more comfortable. We're finding out exactly how much we like living in a place that makes us feel good, even if it takes some planning and effort to get there. We are living the science that is discussed in the pages of this book.

Your PlaceType

We'll define PlaceType more fully in a few pages. The brief explanation: it's how you respond emotionally and cognitively to the physical environment based on your personality.

It's easy to get caught up in what other people are doing and stop designing your home to support you and your life. When television programs and magazine ads are encouraging you to fill your home with bright colors, or modernist furniture, or whatever else is the "décor of the day," it can be difficult to design based on who you are as a person, what's important to you, and what will support your daily life. Designing for PlaceTypes helps you keep yourself and the people with whom you share your home on track toward your goals.

Lots of homes in North America today are built with, or redeveloped with, an open plan, for example. The people whose PlaceTypes are supported by open-plan type layouts are generally pretty vocal, so many architects and contractors have decided that there's no reason to build anything but open plan. However, many PlaceTypes are much, much happier in the sort of "closed-plan" home where specific people and processes (such as cooking) have their own spaces, generally separated from each other with floor-to-ceiling walls and firmly closing doors. The solution for people who own open plan but need closed is rehabbing to support their PlaceType.

Why Think about Design?

Being in appropriately designed places makes it much more likely we'll be happy—along with healthy, wealthy (at least in spirit), and wise. The design of the space we're in has a direct and powerful influence on our mood—literally. When we're in a good mood we think more broadly—which means, for example, that we get along better with other people and are more clever at solving problems and effective at making decisions. We're more creative when we're in a good mood. Basically, when we're in a good mood, positive things are more likely to happen. The design options we'll discuss will make it more likely that when you're in a particular area, you'll be in a better mood.

Stress degrades our physical, emotional, and cognitive well-being, so it's something we'll also often talk about eliminating whenever we can via design.

The influence that design has on your psychological state is the reason that design matters.

CHAPTER 2

UNDERSTANDING THE BASICS OF ENVIRONMENTAL PSYCHOLOGY

Environmental psychology has identified ways that aspects of the environment around us consistently influence how we experience the physical world.

Applying what environmental psychologists have learned about design makes certain types of experiences, thoughts, etc., more probable, but does not definitively determine mental states or actions. Also, the implications of what's going on around us do add up to make a particular mood more likely, but there are other nonphysical influences on what we ultimately think and do. For example, a calming bedroom design won't relax you if you've just heard the exciting news that you're about to become a parent, but it makes it likely that you'll be cooler and more collected when you hear that news than you'd be otherwise.

This book is geared toward interested general readers, so references for the scientifically-derived information that follows aren't included in the text; if you'd like more information about topics covered and the sources of findings presented, please take a look at the Recommended Readings noted at the end of the book.

Designing for Our Ancient Selves

Our sensory apparatus—our eyes, skin, nose, ears, and taste buds—developed eons ago, and the same sorts of sensory experiences that were positive during our early days as a species continue to calm us and boost our mood.

Being in certain sorts of spaces helped us survive long ago, and looking at the same types of places today is good for us mentally.

Seeing nature scenes through windows or in realistic images helps us restock our levels of mental energy after we've depleted them by concentrating for a while, whether on writing code, deciphering the directions for a complicated handicraft project, or something else. They also help us feel less stressed. Nature views help us feel calmer, boost our cognitive performance, and make us more likely to get along better with others, for example. Psychology-wise, the "best" scenes look as if we could step into them and seem to extend far into the distance. We enjoy seeing rolling hills, for example, and clumps of trees that we might, if we are nimble and quick enough, scamper up to escape trouble. Green is key; arid landscapes are not desirable, at least psychologically, and neither are jungles. If you are building a home or office or landscaping one, you can create these sorts of views through your windows. If you're not going to be building or landscaping, add some art or photographs of nature, as they'll also work well.

Green is key.

Looking at water is particularly good for de-stressing and restocking our mental resources and energy levels. "Manmade" water, say a fountain with gently moving water, works as well as a stream. The effort of adding a fountain to an enclosed courtyard without plants, or to a desktop, is quickly earned back via pleasant feelings.

All the views we have in a space aren't outdoors, and all interior views are definitely not created equal. The best ones are those in which we have our backs against something that seems to protect us (such as a wall, a high-backed chair, or a sturdy plant) and where we have a view out over the world around us. People in a conversation niche with a built-in bench tucked into a workplace hallway have this sort of view. Someone perched on a window seat does, too. The first seats taken in seat-yourself restaurants are in booths and have a view of the restaurant's entry. This fondness for protected seats with a view seems tied to our evolutionary past—at one time when our species was young, perches on tree branches high above the ground may have provided the situational awareness we needed to survive.

For practical and aesthetic reasons, not all of the furniture in your home should be placed against the walls. Putting all of the furniture against the walls restricts how you can use a space and can mean that people trying to talk to each other find themselves at uncomfortable distances. So put something solid behind seats that "float" in the middle of a room, because their backs are more than a couple of feet from walls. You have a range of options for that "protective" element, but the key is to keep any of those hypothetical rear-approaching evildoers about an arm's length away—a credenza behind a couch does that. Try to place your furniture so that as few seated people as possible have their backs to hallways or walkways.

Being able to see a long way makes us feel comfortable in our homes.

In nature, if we feel safe, we can see far into the distance, and being able to see a long way makes us feel comfortable in our homes. Try to position some seats in your home so that people sitting in them can see from one room into the next, and, if possible, through a window to see outside by carefully positioning furniture and opportunistically looking for spaces in your homes with views. Having views through your home is possible, even if you're not living in an open plan. Precisely placing some chairs enables people to have long views through a home even if there are plenty of walls. Some PlaceTypes are more comfortable when they have more audio and visual separation from others; if it turns out you're in one of those groups, position screens or install doors so you have some control over others' long views of you.

Things move in nature, but when something moves inside most of the places we design, generally, it's on its way to crashing to the floor. A mobile, wall hanging, or window curtain that drifts in a gentle air-conditioning or heating current near the ceiling adds comforting motion to a space; it's reminiscent of breezes moving through long-ago meadows on wonderful sunny days. If the air-conditioning or heating currents in your home make you think more of hurricanes than drifting butterflies, reposition mobiles or flex sculptures etc. so they move in a window draft or the current of air behind someone walking through an area instead. Daylight in a space will naturally create a sense of movement as shadows change position during the day.

Personality fine-tunes how we respond to seeing other people, but it's generally true that seeing other humans revs us up. We needed to work together to survive long ago, and that early work was often physically demanding. Our nervous systems continue to respond accordingly, boosting our energy level when we see others, as if after their appearance we'll soon be chasing prey or lifting boulders. If you're creating a public sort of space that'll be visited by people with all sorts of personality profiles, build in some screens—things that people cannot see through—to improve visitors' experiences.

Sensory Experiences

COLORS ON SURFACES

Often, fears of making a mistake lead people to paint their walls white or beige and select "safe" colors for furniture, for example, browns that won't show dirt or wear. Choosing colors without information about the psychological consequences of selections made can indeed be intimidating. Different PlaceTypes are supported particularly well by certain color schemes, as described in individual PlaceType write-ups; we will review some general information about color here.

Homeowners have the freedom to paint interior walls whatever colors they choose; all are free to pick the colors that appear on their furniture, rugs, carpets, etc.

The first thing to know about color is that it has three elements: hue, saturation, and brightness.

- A hue is a set of wavelengths we categorize into the same group. Red is a hue, and so are orange, yellow, green, blue, and purple. There are multiple shades of red and orange, for example. Cultures assign meanings to hues, and those associations make some hues good choices for some spaces and not so good options in others.

- Saturation is how pure a color is. Emerald green is more saturated than sage green, and pumpkin oranges are more saturated than smoky shades of orange. Colors that are less saturated seem a little grayer than saturated ones.

- Brightness is how much white seems to be mixed into a color—you could think of brightness as roughly synonymous with lightness. Colors that are brighter have more white mixed into them, so baby blue is lighter than a sapphire blue.

In North America, some of the associations we have to hues are:

- *Blue* is linked to trustworthiness, competence, and dependability, so if you are a consultant who will participate in video conference calls from your at-home desk, paint the wall that will be seen as you speak blue. Blue is also linked more strongly with environmental responsibility than any other color.

- *Yellow* is simultaneously associated with the sun and with cowardice and treachery.

- *Orange* is linked to being a good value.

- *Green* is a shade we associate with nature, environmental responsibility, and rebirth (think: spring).

- *White* is a color that we generally link to being modern as well as to cleanliness, purity, and honesty.

- *Purple* is tied to sophistication.

- *Black* is linked to power, high cost, sophistication, formality, and death.

- *Brown* is associated with ruggedness.

Research has tied seeing certain hues to very particular psychological outcomes:

- When we look at the color *green*, we're more likely to think creatively.

- Seeing even a small amount of *red* briefly degrades our ability to think analytically.

- Looking at the color *red* gives us a burst of brute physical strength, so it may be a good option for the wall behind the washing machine or the one you see while lifting weights. However, looking at red won't help with physical tasks that require specialized skills, such as hitting a tennis ball, or with an activity that requires strength over an extended period of time, such as riding a stationary bicycle.

- Viewing *red* also raises how energized we feel, generally.

- *Red* color signals "danger" and that cautious behavior is in order.

- Heterosexual people who see someone of the opposite gender against a *red* background think that other person is more attractive and desirable than when the same person is viewed against a different colored background.

- Looking at pink, particularly the color of Pepto-Bismol, is very calming.

- Seeing the color *pink* makes women feel more optimistic, and people generally associate the color pink with optimism.

Colors can be warm or cold, and their "temperature" matters—a lot:

- Warm colors are ones that you're likely to see in a roaring fire: reds, oranges, and yellows. Cool ones wouldn't be out of place in an ice cave: blues and greens, for example. Neutral colors like beiges, grays, browns, and even whites can be warmer or cooler. If you're trying to tell if a neutral color or a purple is warm or cool, hold it against a surface that you know to be warm or cool, such as a wall painted orange or a wall painted green—you'll know immediately if the sample is in the same "temperature" as the known surface. Cool colors such as a blue can be relatively warmer or cooler just as an orange can be relatively warmer or cooler. For the purposes of the points that follow, however, all oranges, yellows, and reds can be thought of as warm colors and all blues and greens can be seen as cool ones.

- When we're in a warm-colored space, we actually do feel warmer than we do when we're in an otherwise identical cool-colored space. The difference in apparent temperature is slight but enough in many cases to drive us to feeling just right, or too hot or too cold. If you live in an area where cool winter weather is more of a concern than summer heat, paint the entryway to your home or office a warm color. Or do you make your home in Miami or Caracas or some other place where summer heat is more of an issue than winter cold? Do the reverse, paint your entryway blue. We also expect warmer colored surfaces to be physically warmer than cooler colored ones.

- People seen against warm colors seem a little friendlier, so a warm color is a good option for anywhere you plan to hang out with others.

- People who have cool colors behind them seem more powerful, while people with warm colors behind them seem less powerful. Also, people in spaces where cooler colors predominate feel more powerful than those in spaces featuring warm colors. These links to power are important in offices.

- Warm colors do make it more likely we'll feel hungry. This is a bad thing if you or someone you live with fights a daily battle with calories, but a very good thing if you are feeding a three-year-old who finds all foods, particularly ones you prepare, too disgusting to eat.

- Time seems to pass more slowly in rooms featuring warm colors and more quickly in ones that feature cool shades. These effects can be important in areas where people will need to wait or where they may not enjoy spending time.

- We're drawn toward warm colors, so they're great shades for the ends of long hallways that people need to walk down or for the wall behind a reception desk.

Cold color   Warm color

Colors can also be bright or dark. As mentioned earlier, brighter colors seem to have more white mixed into them than darker colors do, they could also be thought of as lighter colors:

- Spaces with lighter colored walls seem larger than ones with darker colored walls, even if their square footage is the same. If a wall is painted a lighter color, it seems farther away than when it is painted a darker color. The way that color affects apparent distance can be used to "right-shape" rooms that seem to have odd or undesirable dimensions. For example, make a very long and narrow room seem less oblong by painting the two walls that are farther from each other darker colors.

- Ceilings that are lighter colors seem farther from the floor than ceilings that are darker colors. Ceilings also seem higher when the walls are lighter colors than when they're darker.

- We feel more comfortable when the darkest color in a space is on the floor under our feet, the lightest one is over our heads, and intermediary shades connect the two—this is the way colors are often distributed in nature. The ground is often a dark color, for example, and we stand on it. A dark rug on a white or very light-colored floor makes people feel more comfortable.

- When people are estimating the weight of an object, they are likely to feel that it weighs less if it's a lighter color and more if it's a darker one. Putting darker colors closer to the earth, lower on a wall, or on a piece of furniture, etc., and utilizing lighter colors higher up makes whatever is being viewed seem more stable.

- The same color paint will seem to be a darker if it's painted on a surface with more texture.

Bright color   Dark color

Humans generally prefer to look at some hues and aren't that keen on seeing others.

Across the planet, people are more likely to tell you that blues are their favorite colors than any other shades. That makes blues good options for walls if you are planning on selling your home soon.

Yellows, particularly very yellowy greens are the least popular colors worldwide.

It's important to use preferred colors in a space whenever possible, because when we're seeing preferred colors, smelling preferred smells, etc., we're more likely to be in a good mood, which makes it more likely that we'll be friendlier to other people, be better at problem-solving, and think more creatively, for starters, as discussed earlier.

Our minds don't work as well in spaces filled with shades of gray and white; we're so bored by them that our minds drift toward unpleasant thoughts. Humans find gray and white areas less pleasant places to be than ones that feature greens, blues, reds, oranges, purples, and even yellows.

When we see more saturated colors, we feel more stimulated, and brighter colors put us in a more upbeat mood. Colors that are not very saturated but are relatively bright are relaxing—a light sage green is an example of a familiar shade that meets these criteria. Not very saturated but bright colors are also good choices for places where people need to concentrate. To feel more invigorated, use colors that are really saturated but not very bright, like jewel tones—the color of a perfect rich emerald, for example. The bluish shade on the walls in the cover photo for this book is relaxing to look at, while the blue upholstery on the chair is a more energizing shade to view.

To structure future discussions of colors, we can use the following color family names:

> Neutrals: The colors of sand, clouds, and light-colored stones

> Hazy colors: Deeper grays and khaki greens

> Pastels: Light colors and saturated shades

> Jewel tones: Think sapphires, emeralds, rubies, and the jewel of all fruit, eggplants

> Naturals: Greens and the less saturated and bright shades of more subdued flowers

> Metallics: Shiny copper and brass colors

If looking at particular colors brings an intense association to mind, use that color only when that mental message is desirable within the intended context. You may link a particular shade of yellow with marvelous times your family had on your grandmother's front porch because yellow vines grew along the walls there. That yellow should be in your living room. Do you have pleasant memories related to the distinctive blue on the inside walls of the church where you were married? Make sure to use that color somewhere in your home. If you have intense negative associations to a color, don't use it in your home or office even if it's trendy, or even if something that you're shopping for is less expensive in that color. Color-memory links are made in a primordial part of our brain, and you will never be able to ignore or change negative associations.

If you're color-blind, you should ask a friend what color something is in important situations, such as when you're putting together an office that others will visit, so you don't inadvertently signal something undesirable. If you are color-blind, you can still judge the saturation and brightness of various colors. Choose colors that are brighter and less saturated when the goal is relaxation and ones that aren't as bright and are more saturated when you want to get a boost of energy from the world around you.

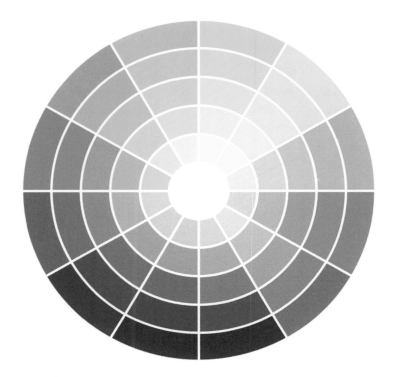

Colors Together and Patterns

Plenty of walls are painted a single color, and lots of sofas are covered in plain upholstery in only one shade, but not all of them. Scientists have also researched how the color combinations and patterns we see on our walls, sofas, floors, duvet covers, and more influence what's going on in our heads.

Some color combinations seem more pleasant to our eyes than others. If you plan to use colors together in a space, assemble samples of all of them and attach them to a piece of board or heavy paper. Look at the planned combinations in a variety of lights to make sure they blend as well in practice as they do in theory.

Using slightly different tints of one color in a space can be relaxing, except if that one color is white/beige, as noted above. Non-white/beige monochrome environments can be good choices for in-home spas or meditation areas, for example.

When used together, colors across the color wheel from each other make us feel more energized (don't forget the effects of saturation and brightness), and this effect is intensified if the colors used are very different in saturation and brightness. Reds and greens are across the color wheel from each other, and so are blues and oranges as well as yellows and purples. Pairs of colors beside each other on the color wheel (for example, purples and blues, blues and greens, greens and yellows, yellows and oranges, oranges and reds, and reds and purples) have the opposite effect on us when we use them together. It's more pleasant when colors used together have approximately equal saturation levels but have a range of different brightness levels.

But what about the patterns we see on rugs, upholstery, wallpapers, and elsewhere? What's best to choose when?

- Sometimes lines are curvier, other times they're straighter. Paisleys feature lots and lots of curving lines and teardrop-like shapes, for example, while plaids are heavy on straight lines arrayed at pointy angles to each other, along with squares and rectangles of color. Paisleys are more curvilinear, while plaids are more rectilinear. We generally are more relaxed by patterns and objects with more curves and more energized by those that are straighter and "pointier." We have the same response to curved and straight lines whether they're in patterns on surfaces or if they determine the shapes of furniture or other objects.

Paisley   Plaid

- Curvier lines and forms are associated with women, femininity, friendliness, and comfort, while more angular ones are linked to men, masculinity, action, strength, and efficiency. Rectilinear patterns and shapes in furniture, moldings, and elsewhere are good for exercise zones and laundry rooms; curvy ones are best for nurseries. A pattern that's a mix of curvy and straight elements will be more or less relaxing, depending on which elements are more plentiful.

- Small size patterns on wallpapers, etc., are the ones most of us like best. These patterns will repeat more times in a space than larger patterns. A small size pattern on wallpaper might feature daisies that are two inches across or smaller; a large size pattern could include daisies larger than that, for example.

- Moderately complicated patterns are preferred to more complex ones and are also those that are most pleasant to look at. These patterns use just a few shapes, although those two or three shapes might be of several sizes and a similar number of hues. A pattern of moderate visual complexity might use circles and squares of a few different sizes and colors on a neutral color background, with about half of the background visible. One alternative with moderate visual complexity would be a pattern that uses several different flower shapes in several darker shades of pink on a light violet background. A few more examples: a Navaho rug has moderate visual complexity, and a Persian rug has high visual complexity.

- Rug patterns can be used to make hallways seem shorter. If two different patterns or textures are used in a corridor, or one asymmetrical pattern is used and that pattern sometimes seems more to the left and at other times seems to be more to the right along the length of a hallway, the hall will seem shorter. If distances are perceived as shorter, people are more likely to move forward, so this information can be used to encourage trips down hallways, for example.

- Visual symmetry, which is often linked with formality, has several forms: reflected and rotated, for example. With reflected symmetry, the shapes are found on either side of a straight line, but their position is reversed. If the image is duplicated on either side of a vertical line, for example, whatever is on the left side of the image on the left side of that vertical line is mirrored on the right side of the image when it's on the right side of that same vertical line. With rotated symmetry, items are repeated around a central hub, the way spokes repeat around the center of a wheel. Humans generally prefer symmetrical patterns, graphics, and artwork compared to asymmetrical options and find them more beautiful. They also prefer symmetrical architecture to asymmetrical spaces. Seeing something that's symmetrical is also likely to improve our mood.

- We'd rather look at horizontal and vertical lines than diagonal ones. Also, diagonal lines that start on the lower left and move to the upper right (ascending lines, ones like this /) are linked in our minds with relatively higher activity levels than diagonals that are higher on the left and lower on the right (ones like this \); these descending diagonals are linked in our minds to relaxation. Ascending lines are better for exercise areas and descending ones for meditation spaces, for example.

Ascending diagonal lines   Descending diagonal lines

- A common color or shape can coordinate various patterns and design elements (such as wallpapers and carpets).

Light

How a space is lit has a major effect on our mood. Natural light is as welcome to a human as it is to a begonia. The light that flows through windows helps us keep our circadian rhythms in sync with the world around us. When they're out of sync, we feel like we're jet-lagged, we grow tense, and our level of well-being plummets.

When we're in a space at least partially lit with natural light, we think more broadly—so we are more apt to be creative, better at solving problems, and better at getting along with others. Position curtains to let in as much daylight as possible, or consider taking them down altogether. Window blinds that roll up or move completely to the side of a window can provide privacy when needed but don't block sunlight when they're rolled up.

Be mindful of glare if you forgo the curtains. Glare can counter all of the good effects that flow from bathing your rooms in sunlight. Sheer curtains can help keep the glare down at different times of day, and so can judicious use of shiny finishes; with fewer shiny surfaces, there is less glare. Some PlaceTypes find shiny things more desirable than others do, but even people who relish shine should plan a space to keep it glare free.

Just like colors, light can be either warm or cool. When we talk about research on colored light, we're discussing investigations of subtle gradations in the light experienced, not those garish red, blue, green, and orange bulbs sold at Halloween and Christmas time. Those odd-colored bulbs distort social interactions; it is thought that is because they make everyone's skin seem to be odd colors. They aren't something you'd want to use in your home or office.

The packages that most light bulbs come in today are labeled warm or cool. If you have some older bulbs hanging around and they're marked only in degrees Kelvin, warm bulbs have a temperature of about 2,700 K(elvin), while light seems cool at about 4,000 or more degrees Kelvin. Warm light is best for relaxing, thinking creatively, and getting along with others, while cooler light is ideal for alertness, concentrating, and analytical reasoning. Our memories also work better under relatively cooler light as compared to warmer light. Researchers have found, for example, that we tend to be in a better mood in warmer light (around 2,700 K) than we are in cooler light (around 6,000 K) at about the intensity of light generally found in offices.

- Warm light in your living room is a good idea—which won't surprise you if you've ever lit a gathering with candles or a fire.

- What should you do about light color in your office, home, or elsewhere? The answer clearly depends. If you're a poet or an accountant (the latter field being one in which creative accounting sometimes leads to jail time), choosing a light color doesn't seem to be a problem, as the advantageous choice is clear; when your occupational success clearly depends on creative or analytical thinking, light bulb color selection is easy. It may be best for you, however, to have both warm and cool lights in your office and to turn one type or the other on at a time, with the color selected depending on what you're trying to accomplish.

- Another consideration: surface colors look best under light colors in the same temperature family—warm surface colors generally look best in warm light and cool surface colors in cooler light. Cross temperature design can make surface colors seem muddy or like they need a good scrub. Since the saturation and brightness of a surface color determine its emotional effect, it's generally best to pick a surface hue after deciding on the light color that makes it more likely you'll think the sorts of thoughts you've planned for a space. After you've selected a light color, you can select a warm or cool surface color to coordinate with that light temperature.

- Warmer lights are generally preferred during the evening (which makes sense because in our evolutionary past, fires would have been a comforting presence at night), while cooler lights win out during the day. Having a mix of bulbs in a room means you can light a space in different ways at different times.

- When you're using warm lights, for full effect, they should be placed lower than the top of your head and be focused on tabletops and other horizontal surfaces. Energizing light, that is, cooler light, should be placed higher than the top of your head and should flood the walls and splash your ceiling with light.

- Night-lights should be red or amber shades because those are less disruptive to our circadian rhythms.

Light can be darker and lighter, too. Professionals have all sorts of fancy tools to tell how bright or dark a light is, and everyone else just has eyes. What you need to know is that as light gets brighter, our energy levels climb. Intensely bright light works well for operating heavy machinery and doing surgery. The light of a single candle is great for a quiet conversation. Light-colored walls and glossy surfaces make lights seem a little brighter, and that means they are more energizing, something to remember when you're picking materials for surfaces. Lights on dimmers or with a few preset settings allow you to select the light intensities that work for you in a particular moment.

Humans are most comfortable in spaces with certain distributions of light. Allover bright or dark is not what makes us feel good. Lighter colors on walls makes spaces seem bigger, and positioning pot lights in ceilings and other similar "luminaires" so that they bathe walls in light also makes a space seem larger—which can be a good thing or not, depending on the true size of the space and what's planned.

"Dappled" light is a big hit with humans; we feel good when we bask in it. Dappled light is slightly darker in some places and slightly lighter in others, just like the light that comes through the branches of a leafy tree on a sunny day. Tabletop lamps are better options in socializing areas than overhead lights that bathe an entire room in a blanket of light that is the same color and intensity everywhere. Pools of light also create zones in a space. Those zones may be dedicated to a particular task, such as dining, playing cards, or meeting to discuss a new advertising campaign or other brainstorming , and that's a good thing. They indicate a territory, and when we're in a territory we control, we're happier, more relaxed, and more productive. People in the same light zone tend to socialize with each other.

Science has shown that it's useful to subtly vary the color and intensity of the light in your home and workplace to mirror the color and intensity cycles of light outdoors. This helps keep your circadian rhythms in sync with the world around you and your mood good. That means warmer light is best during morning and evening hours and cooler light works well midday. Light outdoors is brightest at noon, and light inside should also be most intense then.

Visual Complexity (Be Brave, Read This Section)

The visual complexity of an environment has a significant effect on how we feel when we're there. Visual complexity is determined by the number of colors, shapes, and other visual elements present and their symmetry and organization.

The bottom line of all of the research that's been done is that it's generally best for humans to be in spaces with moderate visual complexity. We're most relaxed and comfortable in a space with moderate visual complexity—too much or too little visual complexity is unpleasant and makes us feel tense. Our brains also work better in spaces with moderate visual complexity, even when we're as young as three years old. We also prefer art and visual patterns (say, on wallpaper) with moderate visual complexity.

Spaces that are more than moderately complex energize us. Higher energy levels are better in an exercise area, for example.

"Moderate visual complexity" is a phrase that has no real meaning to the humans on the planet who aren't environmental psychologists, so examples are in order. A residential interior created by Frank Lloyd Wright has moderate visual complexity. The interior of the Meyer May home, designed by Wright, is moderately complex visually, and so is Taliesin in Wisconsin, another Wright-designed home and one he lived in himself. Images of both of these homes are available online.

If you are trying to create moderate visual complexity, the best way to determine the complexity of a space is to visualize one of Wright's residential interiors, or another a space known to have moderate visual complexity, and then mentally compare the complexity of the two. This may sound like a dubious way to proceed, but it works.

The number of patterns on surfaces makes the single largest contribution to how visually complex a place is. To manage complexity, all of the patterns in any room or other defined space should always use the same select set of colors. Patterns used together should all feature the same few shades of brown and blue, for example. To qualify as "moderately complex visually," a space needs to feature just a few patterns: *few* being two or three if the third is very similar to one of the first two. So, the upholstery on your sofa and your curtains can be patterned, but that's it. Maybe a rug can be patterned if the upholstery and curtain patterns are very similar—however, no patterned wallpaper. Some PlaceTypes can tolerate slightly higher levels of visual complexity; read on to see if you have one of those PlaceTypes. Patterns that are themselves moderately visually complex feature a limited number of families of hues and shapes, three of each.

Places that are more complex visually also have lots of stuff scattered across their horizontal surfaces. Furniture, which rests on the floor, is some of this stuff. Photographs in lovely frames perched on sideboards, glass sculptures inherited from Aunt Milly, and wonderful artworks created by Teddy in preschool also contribute to visual complexity.

The number of patterns on surfaces makes the single largest contribution to how visually complex a place is.

It's important that you have things around you that have meaning for you—just not too many of them at any one time. Most of the horizontal furniture surfaces in your home should not have anything on them. Since there are fewer feet of horizontal space in smaller homes than larger ones, and since every room needs a few things that show that it's yours—photographs, souvenirs from travels, items inherited from your grandmother—it's not possible to set an exact number of the horizontal furniture surfaces in your home that should not have anything resting on them. To find what level of "horizontal coverage" works best for you, take all of your mementos, photos, etc., off of the tabletops, bookshelves, and so forth in a space. Books can stay on bookshelves, but remove all the other stuff that's found its way onto the shelves. This process will probably make you feel tense. Start to add back single items to the furniture surfaces one by one, and wait for a minute or so between additions. When you find yourself breathing normally again, stop adding items. You've found your object-space happy zone.

Wall art and photographs should not cover more than 50 percent of the wall spaces, not counting the wall space behind furniture. To keep visual complexity in check, when 50 percent of the wall space will be covered, the images shown should be few and simple—a swirl of blue representing a wave, not a detailed painting of that wave showing sea creatures and vegetation, for example. If a detailed image is used on a wall, fewer images should be used and more wall space left blank. Mirrors are equivalent to a very complex image.

Clutter is the stack of magazines you plan to read, the pile of pictures waiting for frames, the reports that need to be filed, and the four sweaters lying across the first chair you pass as you enter your home. It is stuff you want and have good reasons to keep, but that just hasn't found its way to its where it needs to be. Empty pizza boxes and dishes that need to be washed are trash and cleaning that need to get done; they need to be dealt with for biological reasons.

The reason why clutter is so stressful for humans is because it amps up the visual complexity in our world. Keeping clutter in check is a reason to make sure you have enough drawers and cabinets and to ensure that no one can see what's in them. If you place something in a drawer or cabinet but you can still see it in its new resting place, you've accomplished nothing clutter-wise.

Clutter reduces well-being and degrades professional cognitive performance. People are in better moods in places that are more organized than disorganized. Clutter and visual disorder have an insidious effect. Clutter and disorganization degrade the self-control of all who encounter them as well as people's ability to follow rules. If you're trying to avoid the Halloween candy that made its way into your home at the end of October, your odds of success fall with each wayward sock, file folder, and magazine cluttering up your kitchen. If you want people entering your home to neatly stow their coats and boots, make sure there are compartments, shelves, or something similar in place so that your entry space seems orderly. The same is true for laundry rooms—if you want people to wipe up little spills and clean out lint traps, make sure your laundry room is designed in such a way—with cupboards, for example—to make it possible to keep it well-ordered. When we're in more orderly spaces, we also seem to more thoughtfully evaluate information.

Once you clear the clutter, parts of your home that you haven't really seen for years will become visible. If they're bedraggled, un-bedraggle them—nothing's more demoralizing that living in a place that's seen better days. Paint walls that are chipped or dirty, add a slipcover over the worn sofa, and introduce a few (not too many, remember the hassle of getting rid of that clutter) throw pillows.

Too little going on around us is as upsetting as too much. Spaces can definitely be too stark for comfort. The environments where we developed our current crop of sensory tools featured multiple colors, a gentle hum of activity, and changing light levels and patterns of shadows, for example. So should the home and workspaces you use today.

Art

Art can give us a positive psychological boost. It can send out messages that let others know what we value about ourselves—while it reminds us of the same things. An historic photograph can signal a longstanding connection to an area, an organization, or a family, and a painting of a seagull can signal an attachment to the sea or animals or sailing, for example. The full set of stuff you've added to your home and office determines the messages sent. Art depicting nature was discussed earlier in this chapter during the review of how our ancient experiences influence where we live best now.

Realistic images of nature can to a great extent compensate for the stress we feel being in a space without windows—making them a particularly good choice for spaces such as tiny powder rooms. Realistic nature art has also been linked to enhanced creative thinking.

With art, we prefer the familiar but aren't very enthusiastic about pieces that are entirely predictable and boring. The same is true for interior and product design and architecture—the familiar with a slight twist is most likely to please us.

All that was reported earlier about how humans respond to colors and shapes also applies to art. Abstract images with more curvy than straight lines in them and which feature colors that are not very saturated but are relatively bright are calming to view, for example. Pieces that have more straight lines than curvy ones with more saturated, not so bright elements are more energizing to view. The research on lines and shapes can be applied to sculpture as well.

Human beings are more likely to think creatively when they're feeling nostalgic, and art, particularly photographs, can be used inspire nostalgia. When we experience awe—and the same item/view/space can awe us over and over again—we feel less rushed and more satisfied with life, and are more likely to be helpful to others, so an awe inspiring item in a family room or office can be a good addition. Something inspires awe when it is large or exhibits superb workmanship, for example. Art can make us feel awed, but so can an inlay pattern on a floor or a light fixture or the stone on a countertop, for instance.

Materials

Filling your home with natural materials such as wood is good for your body and mind. Seeing the grain in wood de-stresses us. No wonder hardwood floors have been popular in homes for so long. Floors aren't the only surfaces where wood grain can sing; furniture and woodwork can show it off, too. Seeing real and artificial wood grain has the same effect on us as long as two things are true: the artificial wood is a really, truly good imitation of natural wood, and the repeat pattern in the artificial wood is random enough so that the same distinctive feature, say a simulated knot, is not repeated in the finished floor or piece of furniture in an unnaturally predictable way. Spaces that feature natural wood have randomly distributed patterns in their wooden surfaces; the same randomness needs to be present in any your home or office if you're using a product with artificial wood grain.

It's great that seeing wood grain de-stresses us because it can be used in lots of spaces where it might be hard to design in window views or grow plants, such as basements. We are also better able to concentrate in spaces featuring wood. Wood ceilings may encourage people to fall asleep more quickly if light bounces off of them. However, it's best if no more than 45 percent of the surfaces in an area are covered with wood. With this amount of wood on view, we're most comfortable and relaxed.

Matte finishes are more relaxing for us to look at than shiny ones, and many natural materials can readily be used with or without a shine.

Matte finishes are more relaxing than shiny ones.

Stones, for example, can be polished or not as desired. So can many styles of tiles and other surface materials. Shiny finishes are, however, preferred over matte finishes.

Information on which materials and finishes off-gas dangerous materials is continually being updated as more related research is done and as new surfaces come onto the market. Visit reliable online data sources, such as the websites of the American Institute of Architects, the American Society of Interior Designers, or the International Interior Design Association for the latest news on healthy materials.

Audio Experiences

Just as professionals travel around with light meters so they can determine how bright a light is, they also have monitors that let them know how loud it is in a space. When sound levels in workplaces get to around forty-five decibels (dB), our lives start to degrade, and, in more public, social situations, the magic volume level that divides happy from stressed listeners is around sixty decibels. How loud is that? The loudness of a whisper or of gently rustling leaves is twenty dB, the sound level in a quiet library is about thirty dB, and that of a quiet room or busier library is forty dB. Forty-five dB is about as loud as a conversation between two people generally gets. The loudness of an alarm clock is eighty dB.

You can influence the soundscapes in your home and workplace by playing music or birdsongs (more on this below) or via rules about who is allowed to talk when. Other soundscape modifications require professionals—for example, adding sound blocking insulation to walls or using acoustic ceiling tiles.

Anything that's relevant or potentially relevant to what we're doing is a distracting noise, and since speech can at any time become relevant, it needs to be monitored and is particularly distracting. Meaningful noise degrades cognitive performance.

Sometimes people are told to ignore people around them who are talking or other uncontrollable sounds, such as water dripping. But humans can't do that—no matter how hard we try. This also seems to be tied to our experiences as a young species, when ignoring others or ignoring a noise might have made us some other creature's lunch. Since we can't ignore conversations around us, it can be particularly important to acoustically isolate offices, bedrooms, home spas, and similar areas by placing them at a distance from noisier zones or adding sound insulating materials to the walls around them. Walls that reach to the lower level of the floor above are much more effective at blocking sounds than walls that reach only to a dropped ceiling. The space between a dropped ceiling and the true ceiling in an area is a sound superhighway, a zone that makes a nearly whispered conversation instantly known to all. To effectively manage sound, it's important to understand when there's a gap between a true ceiling and a dropped ceiling and block it. Echoes have particularly negative effects on our cognitive performance and social behavior; soft surfaces such as rugs and wall hangings can help keep them in check.

It is not your imagination; random noises (as opposed to continuous or predictable ones) really are the most annoying. If a leaky faucet starts to drip intermittently, you need to stop the noise, even if by just putting a face cloth where the water hits the sink. You cannot ignore the sound or "not let it bother you." Any random unpredictable sounds in your house or office need to be acoustically isolated so that they don't destroy the atmosphere you're trying to create. Make sure, for example, that you can't hear the printer that springs randomly into action. It can be worth the costs to invest in heating, ventilation, and air-conditioning (HVAC) systems that don't make unpredictable, distressing noises or to install sound absorbing materials in and around hobby spaces where people will operate power tools.

The fact that most of us can't just turn off our ears also means that we need to add background noise to a space where we want to feel good and think clearly. Research has linked particular attributes of sounds with certain mental states. High-pitched sounds (for example, violins) set our nerves on edge, while ones that are lower in pitch, like a guitar, relax us. Music in a major key boosts our mood, while music in minor keys has the opposite effect.

Our hearts beat in time to the soundscape we're in, and changing the pace at which our hearts are beating is integral to influencing our mood. Faster sounds, whether music or otherwise, energize us, while slower ones calm us. Fast-paced music in a major key makes us feel high in energy and in a good mood, while slower music in a minor key has the opposite effect. We even walk faster when we hear music with more beats per minute. Relaxing music has between 50 and 70 beats per minute, and very relaxing songs like lullabies have 30 to 50 or so beats per minute. Songs with 100 to 130 beats per minute energize us. Not sure how many beats per minute are in the music you enjoy? Google "beats per minute" to find one of the websites that provides exactly this sort of information.

People's brains do their best knowledge-type work when they're in a space where the noise has been cut to a quiet background hum that reminds them they're not the last person on the planet but the words other people are saying aren't clear or loud enough to be understood; this is similar to a relatively quiet office while wearing headphones but not listening to music or anything else through them.

White noise blocks distracting background sounds, while pink noise calms us. Examples of each of these kinds of noise are available online at Wikipedia, and each can be added to a space via online services, as well. White noise has been shown to boost our cognitive performance compared to how well our brains usually work when listening to office type noise.

If white or pink noise, which get their names because of the patterns in their sound waves, seem a little institutional to you, there are other options. It's psychologically better to listen to music you like than music you don't like, but if the people who use a space have very different music preferences, go with classical, nonvocal music, as it's universally positively—well, or at least not negatively—received. Scientists have also learned that when we hear the sorts of birdcalls, gentle water movements, and rustling wind noises found in a temperate zone meadow on a lovely spring day, we immediately feel calmer. These sounds also help us restock our mental processing power after we've depleted it doing knowledge work. Playing nature sounds may sound silly, but it's proven effective in a range of spaces, from doctor's waiting rooms to workplaces to living rooms. Restful and rejuvenating meadow soundtracks are available online.

Don't try to create a place that's completely quiet or quieter than we'd expect—that's just as unnerving to humans as one that's too noisy. Concentrate instead on having the right sorts of sounds fill a space, the ones that help you create desired moods.

The soundscape in your home can, and should, be actively managed. What sounds do you like to hear? Birds singing? Street vendors from Marrakesh? Mozart? The sounds outside your home? Are you one of the few people who isn't driven crazy by the sound of wind chimes? Set up a sound system so you can listen to what you enjoy hearing when you're hanging around at home. Modify your soundscapes so that being inside your home is a different experience in the morning, afternoon, and evening, and at different times of the year.

Scents

Rigorous scientific research has linked particular scents to certain psychological states. It is possible to disperse aromas through a space in multiple ways. Essential oils can be wicked into the air, for example, and scent dispensers can be incorporated into HVAC systems with a professional's assistance.

Smelling pleasant scents has been shown to boost mood.

The scents listed below have their noted effects whether the people smelling them are aware of them or not; the effects linger after the smell fades from perception. The amount of any smell that should to be added to a space needs to be determined via a straightforward onsite experiment, because things like window drafts, exact room volumes, and how well a ventilation system works all have a dramatic effect on whether a particular amount of an odor can be smelled. To conduct the required experiment: dispense a very small amount of an odor into a space. If anyone who enters the area mentions the smell, the amount used needs to be reduced. Ask people who come by about their experiences of being in the space, and cut back the amount of scent in use if it is brought up. Even at the same concentration in the air, some scents are more pungent than others, so each scent needs to be tested individually.

- Smelling pleasant scents has been cross-culturally shown to boost mood. As discussed earlier, when we're in a more positive mood, we're better at problem-solving, thinking creatively, and getting along with others. Pleasant smells reduce stress, and unpleasant smells have the reverse effect.

- If a place is pleasantly scented, we feel we have spent less time there and that it is larger than if the space is unscented.

- A pleasantly scented space seems cleaner and brighter.

- We linger in spaces that smell good to us.

- Smelling scents we link to cleanliness has been linked to better behavior and following rules.

- We are also fairer and more generous in spaces that smell "clean" to us, with clean smells being the scents used in cleaning products in our culture. North Americans associate the distinctive smell of Windex with cleanliness, for example. So, cleaning up before company arrives pays off in more ways than you might have thought.

Scientists have also investigated the implications of smelling particular scents:

- Aromas that have been tied to lower anxiety levels include sweet orange (this refers to the oranges we eat), floral scents (particularly hyacinth and jasmine), and vanilla. The smell of ylang-ylang seems calming.

- Relaxing scents include lemon, mango, and lavender.

- Scents linked to increased alertness: peppermint, common garden sage, and rosemary; coffee countered the effects of sleep deprivation in rats.

- Energizing scents are grapefruit, tangerine, eucalyptus, and peppermint.

- The scent of lavender is linked to helping encourage sleep.

- Scents that boost cognitive performance: cinnamon and vanilla; creativity is linked to coffee (even if no caffeine is actually present or coffee consumed) as well as lemon.

- Scents linked to improved memory function: rosemary, peppermint, and common garden sage.

- Scents to support performing clerical type work include chocolate and coffee.

- The scent of lemon is linked to improving mood while doing knowledge work.

- Lavender is also linked to trusting other people.

Since scents are tested one at a time in labs, the research supports using a single scent in a space.

Certain smells are particularly important to each of us emotionally. You can't change your responses to those scents, so use them to your advantage. If you have relaxing associations with the smell of something, use it to scent your bedroom or wherever else you'd like to feel relaxed, whether this text mentions it or not. If you don't like smelling a scent because you have negative associations with it—maybe your mean Aunt Joan's house smelled like lemon, so you dislike the smell of lemons to this day—then don't use those scents in your home or office, no matter what research has said about them. Scent associations can't be overcome, they just are.

Some people avoid scenting spaces because of allergies. Natural scents can be replaced by artificial ones to overcome this problem. Various brands of artificial scents are made with different ingredients, so you should be able to find one that doesn't trigger whatever allergies are present.

Smelling the same odor in different places or different times when you'll be working on a project puts you in the same mindset in these places and times and helps call the same project-related thoughts and details to consciousness in each space and time, which makes your mind work more efficiently and effectively. The same goes for sounds heard and other sensory experiences. If your home office and your workplace at your firm's headquarters share a scent or other sensory stimulus and continue to do so over time, that consistency will improve your professional performance.

ON-SKIN EXPERIENCES

Scientists have thoroughly probed the ways that our tactile experiences influence how we think and behave.

- How much padding there is on a chair cushion matters in more ways than you might have imagined. People who sit on even relatively slim cushions (about an inch thick) do not drive as hard a bargain when negotiating as people without cushions. The people sitting on the cushions are more flexible—in most families with kids, in particular, cushions all around seem like a great idea. Would you like to make your family meals more pleasant, and discussions of curfews, allowances, and family vacations less onerous? Make sure both parents and kids have cushions between their butts and the dining chairs.

- Researchers have also found that after people touch something that is warm and put it down, they judge others to be more generous and caring than if they've just held something cooler, and they are themselves more generous, trusting, and cooperative than after holding something cooler. Body heat warms some materials faster than others, and not all materials retain heat effectively. Metal surfaces heat up quickly but lose their heat quickly. Wood and leather store heat well.

- When felt, smoother surfaces are linked to femininity and rougher ones to masculinity, and touching a rougher surface is more energizing than feeling a smoother one. When various textures are used together, the effect is energizing.

- Smoother metal is associated with being modern, elegant, and comfortable.

- People tend to prefer staying on the same underfoot texture; if they've been walking on carpet, they're unlikely to move off that carpeted path onto vinyl tiles, for example. Changes in underfoot textures signal to humans that they should pay attention, so changing flooring at the top of stairs, for example, or where there is surfacing around a pool deck is a good idea.

- We walk more slowly on carpet than harder floors, so carpet can be a good choice where you want to keep people moving slowly, to view art, for instance.

- People are more comfortable in places with carpet than vinyl floors and tend to spend more time in those carpeted areas.

- Floors that are shiny may be perceived as slippery, whether they are or are not.

Temperature

Thermostats, whether at home or at work, are often battlegrounds. Some people inevitably want to live and work in warmer temperatures and others in colder ones. Science can help resolve these disputes.

- Keeping indoor spaces around seventy degrees Fahrenheit encourages pleasant social interactions.

- Our minds do their best work when we're in a place that's sixty-eight to seventy-four degrees Fahrenheit, with humidity between 40 and 70 percent and gentle, almost imperceptible ventilation. There are a number of reasons why this temperature may not be achievable, from energy costs to a desire to save the planet by cutting energy use, but when you have options, it's good to know what's likely to work best for the greatest number of people.

- Our hands, feet, and heads are not equally sensitive to heat and cold. Radiant heat focuses heat onto our feet, which makes us feel warmer than if the area around our heads is heated. Air-conditioning ducts up higher do a good job at cooling our heads and therefore making us feel cooler overall.

- It's important that places where you plan to hang out are in the comfort range of temperature overall. When we're comfortably warm (but not hot), we are more sociable.

- We feel cooler when we're alone than when we're with others, so thermostats should be set at higher levels in places where people will spend most of their time alone.

- People are more likely to go along with opinions of others when comfortably warm than when they are comfortably cool, so a family room that's a little warmer but still in the comfortable range might be a good idea when you anticipate potential family squabbles. The same goes for conference rooms at work where negotiations take place.

- Experiencing relatively cooler (but still comfortable) temperatures has been tied to more emotional decision-making and a tendency to select products based on how pleasurable they are to use. In relatively warmer (but still comfortable) temperatures, our decision-making is more rational and utilitarian arguments prevail. You may want to heat or cool spaces you use accordingly to encourage one sort of thinking or another; you might, for example, vary the temperature based on whether you need to make investment decisions or host a family holiday party.

Right-Sizing

Some spaces seem to be just the right size, others seem too big or too small. We're less likely to feel stressed in spaces that seem like they're the right size, which is important because when we're stressed, our cognitive performance and general well-being are reduced and our mood curdles.

- Lighter colored walls make a space seem a little larger, while darker colored walls make it seem a little bit smaller. If you have a bedroom that's just too big to feel comfortably cozy, a darker jewel tone on the walls can be just what you need to make the space feel like it's just the right size. In a tiny powder room, a lighter color on the walls, say a delicate aquamarine, is a better option.

- When a space is a little more brightly lit, it seems a little larger than if the lights are slightly dimmer.

- When a space has a more even distribution of light, it seems larger than if there are variations in the intensity of light in the space, as there are when there are brighter and darker dollops of light on the floor of a room.

- Relatively cooler colored lights (say 4,000K) in a space make it seem a little larger than it does when warmer colored lights (around 2,700K) are used in the same space. If you want a space to seem slightly cozier at some times and slightly larger at others, put different colored light bulbs in different lamps and turn on the ones with the cooler bulbs or the ones with the warmer ones to create the size impression desired.

- Adding a scent associated with a larger, more open space, like the scent of the ocean, to an indoor space makes it seem a little larger, while adding a scent associated with coziness to an area, say the smell of a crackling fireplace, makes the same space seem a little smaller. Adding a smell tied to an open space to a large space can actually make people feel anxious. Adding any scent to a space makes it seem a little larger than it does when it is unscented.

- Installing bookshelves along one wall of a room and then putting only a few things on those shelves will make a space seem larger, even though the book shelves inevitably take up some of the floor space in the room.

- Generally, a space also seems larger when there are more openings such as windows and doors in its walls than when there are fewer. A single window or skylight will make a room seem more spacious. Even very small openings, such as those created when wooden bands are woven together to create interior walls, make a space seem larger.

A single window or skylight will make a room seem more spacious.

- A rectangular room seems larger than a square room that actually has the same number of square feet.

- A room with curved walls seems smaller than a room that actually has the same number of square feet but straight walls (i.e., a more rectilinear floor plan).

- Spaces with lower ceilings—below the about ten-foot height that currently seems desirable in homes—seem smaller than those with higher ceilings even if the areas are actually the same size.

- Spaces on higher floors also seem larger than places with the same number of feet on a lower floor, so if all the floors in your home have the same floor plan, you might decide to move your living areas to the top level so that they will seem a little more spacious.

- Smaller scale patterns, on wallpapers, for example, make a space seem larger, while larger scale prints make it seem smaller.

- Mirrors on walls make a space seem larger.

- A space seems larger if the space from which we enter it is more dimly lit or has smaller windows.

Furniture

Different PlaceTypes leave furniture stores (or their grandmother's attic) with different pieces, but there are fundamentals of furniture management that everyone should consider because they are based in the most basic ways that humans want to interact with each other.

The distances we prefer to be from each other differ from situation to situation; being too close to someone else bothers us, but so does being too far away. Our preferred distances from others vary based on culture and on our relationship with the people we're talking to—but even within a single culture, some people sit closer to each other in any circumstance than others.

To accommodate these slight differences, successful spaces allow people to scoot either themselves or their chairs a few inches closer or farther from other people as they prefer. When chairs are too large to easily move a little, people can still reposition themselves to slightly different distances from other people if their seats are a little wider than they need to be to accommodate those sitting in them. Being able to slightly reposition seats or themselves is also useful when the people sitting are taller or shorter than average, since taller people prefer slightly larger interpersonal distances than shorter people do in the same situation.

It's important that in a seating area there are some chairs that are beside each other, like the seats in the same row on an airplane, and some that are face-to-face, so that when people sitting in them look straight ahead they are looking directly into someone else's eyes. Other chairs should be placed so that they're at right angles to each other, as seats are arranged when people are sitting around the corner from each other at a conference room table. These configurations each work best in a particular type of situation:

- A side-to-side layout is best when a conversation is likely to be extremely stressful or when two men are talking. Think about all of the difficult conversations you've had in cars, and you'll have plenty of examples of when side-to-side discussions worked very well.

- Face-to-face is good for when two women are having a serious conversation, when the reasons you're speaking are social, or when you'll be talking about some topic that isn't likely to increase anyone's blood pressure, such as vegetable gardening.

- Right angle seating unsurprisingly works in situations that might become stressful. When seated this way, people have easy control of whether they have eye contact with each other or not; it's easy to look away briefly to diffuse a situation without seeming rude.

Dining tables are places where socializing is really important. When you're laying out chairs around your dining room table, make sure that there are about thirty-two to thirty-four inches between the middle of the backs of each guest chair, if North Americans will be sitting in those seats. Other cultures have different preferred distances for casual conversation, some closer, some farther away. It's easy to learn about a particular culture's preferred interpersonal distances by Googling the topic. It is possible to make some generalizations, however; for example, when having the same type of conversation, people from Latin America generally stand closer to each other than people from the United States, and Japanese people are generally farther from each other than people from the United States.

Your seated posture—the way that you sit—is related to how you talk with other people. Remember all those dads in 1950s sitcoms who commanded their families from their recliners? When people stretch out in a more open body position while sitting, as they do when they're in a recliner or have their feet on an ottoman, they feel more powerful than if they're sitting the way we do in straight chairs with all our limbs close to our body—and they act accordingly. Depending on what sort of dynamic you want in your home, you may prefer that everyone living in your house be able to recline in the family room, that only parents be able to stretch out, or that no one be able to do so. A benefit of talking to others while reclining: people in reclined postures are apt to think more creatively and get less angry when provoked than people sitting up in a conventional desk chair posture; maybe parents should be issued a pair of recliners before they bring new babies home from the hospital.

All of our mothers were right when they told us that sitting up straight is a good idea in certain circumstances. When we do sit up, we tend to have a more positive view of ourselves than people who are slouching, which can help us plow forward through difficult tasks. This means your office chair and the chairs kids sit in as they do homework should be designed to make it likely that people in them will sit up straight.

If you have a large family room, with ceilings so high that they're comparable to those in a medieval cathedral, you may have decided to invest in oversized furniture. Deciding to match a large-scale room with large-scale furniture can seem like a really good idea. Unfortunately, most of the population is not over six feet tall, and that's about the height required to sit on those high and deep couches and chairs and still have your feet touch the floor. Adults who have grown to a conventional height expect to be able to sit on couches and chairs and be able to put their feet flat on the floor. When they can't they are, technically, "infantilized." That means they feel like children, and that can really distort social interactions. Infantilization is not conducive to building and maintaining positive relationships. Even though the look won't be quite right, it's better to use conventional size furniture than extra-tall and extra-deep pieces in spaces with very high ceilings.

Humans associate height off the ground with power, and when a person has to look down into someone else's eyes to talk with them, socializing and conversations are dramatically affected. People in higher seats have more authority. The eyes of everyone participating in a discussion should be at the same height off the floor whenever possible. This means that stadium type tiered seating has no place in homes or offices; also, people involved in discussions of consequential topics (whether mom should move into a care facility, for example) should not be seated on low chairs or floor cushions if others present are seated in regular height chairs.

When people are gathered around a table, if there's anything that can be construed as a "head of the table" position, the person who sits there will be the leader of the group. A preexisting leader will choose that seat. If there is no preexisting leader, the person who sits there becomes the group leader. If you really want to have everyone at your gatherings have equal status and to make it more likely that they'll all participate in the conversation, you need to seat them at a round table. Round tables that can accommodate more than just a couple of people can be difficult to fit into a dining room, because people have traditionally used rectangular tables, so dining rooms are designed for tables of that shape. It's also hard to fit round conference tables that sit more than just a couple of people into conference rooms, again because of the typical room shape. If you want a leaderless dinner, but you have a rectangular table, move the chairs so that they are arranged along the longer sides of your table with none on the shorter sides. If you've got a square table, make sure that people sitting on all sides of your table will feel equal. For example, centerpieces should not make one side seem to be the place where the leader should sit.

If you want people to make easy eye contact with each other, their chairs have to be arranged so that their eyes are all pointed roughly in toward the center of a circle. Often, chairs in family rooms are arranged so that the people sitting in them have great views of the television, but not of each other. Family dynamics suffer. Too much eye contact is stressful for some, and, in those cases, it works out well if there's something to which people in those centrally-oriented chairs can gracefully divert their eyes when the togetherness gets to be too much. This "eye diversion" might be a fish tank, flower arrangement, hanging mobile, or cheerfully blazing fireplace. Fireplaces and fires still have an important place in humans' hearts. They are highly valued in Western homes, even though we're unlikely to need them for heat. Among the middle class, homes with more than one fireplace are prized.

If you want easy eye contact, chairs should be pointed roughly in toward the center of a circle.

Modern humans spend a lot of time sitting, and that may not be healthy for us. Sitting can harm our health for reasons other than what it does to our waistlines. Being seated has been associated with a decrease in mental well-being, which means it can harm your mood and mental performance. Try to lay out your home and office so that you have to walk around to get things done. A bonus of walking around is that doing so enhances creative thinking. You can also install a sit-stand desk in your office so that you can spend part of your work time standing up. If a sit-stand desk is unavailable in your area or is too expensive, put two desks near each other in your office, one with a work surface at conventional height, the other with a work surface that is a comfortable height at which to work when you're standing up; alternatively, build a lightweight, easily moveable higher work surface for yourself using materials such as very sturdy empty boxes.

How furniture is arranged in a bedroom can also make us feel protected, or not. The best place to position a bed is with view of the door, but as far as possible from that door. The bed should be located so that someone lying there can see when the door is open. If space allows, it's also desirable to position the bed so that the door itself keeps anyone entering from seeing the person in bed until the door is fully open.

Mirrors are a particularly interesting sort of shiny surface.

- The shine on mirrors and the way that they complicate the environment by visually duplicating it can add pep and vigor to a space while simultaneously making it seem larger.

- Seeing yourself in a mirror also leads you to think a little differently. People are more apt to follow society's rules when they can see themselves in a mirror, so they are a good choice for places in your home where you're worried about dishonest behavior, like a space in your home where a teenager may be tempted to do something that's not a good idea with a friend. You might also choose to use a shiny, mirror-like surface somewhere outside your home to keep down littering or to keep people on their toes while they're deciding which bin is the right one for their recyclables.

- We are also less likely to eat unhealthy food when we see ourselves in a mirror; our unhealthy choices don't taste as good to us when we can see ourselves in a mirror as they do when we can't. However, people eating alone think food generally tastes better when they can see themselves in a mirror, and they eat more, so a mirror can be a good addition to the dining area of an older person who is not eating as much as they should.

- Mirrors can ricochet daylight through a space so that sunlight's benefits are available in more areas, but be aware of the need to avoid glare.

Architectural Features

There are aspects of your home which are difficult to change that influence you psychologically. These are things such as where walls, ceilings, and windows are located, and research on this subject is useful if you are building a new home or extensively remodeling an existing one.

Ceilings hang above our heads, so it's no surprise that how they are situated has a significant influence on how we experience a space.

- Ceiling height is a clue to how formal a situation is. Higher ceilings, particularly the fifteen- or twenty-foot-high ceilings often found in public spaces, tell us to use our best manners and *behave*. If you live in a house with a family room that has immensely high ceilings, you have probably already noticed that people hanging out there aren't as chummy as you'd anticipated they'd be.

- Ceilings that are approximately ten feet high seem to hit a sweet spot in terms of human experience—not so high that they cause us to act in a formal way and not so low that we feel claustrophobic and tense.

- We prefer to be in spaces where the ceilings are flat or only gently sloping. A gently sloping ceiling rises or falls four feet for every twelve feet measured along the floor of a room.

- The best solutions for ceilings that are "too high" are to either lower the ceilings in particular areas of the room or install some sort of canopy about nine to ten feet above where people will be seated. Another potential fix would be a chair with some sort of top that extends out over a seated person's head, which will make that individual feel more comfortable under an over-tall ceiling.

- When we're in a space with a ten-foot-high ceiling, we think more broadly and creatively than when we're in a space with an eight-foot ceiling. If we're thinking broadly, we also get along better with others, so ten-foot ceilings may cause us to be at our social best. In an area with eight-foot ceilings, we do better on tasks that require us to focus on details.

Room shape also has psychological implications:

- We prefer to be in rooms that are square as opposed to rectangular.

- We like to be in rooms where the walls meet at angles of ninety degrees or more.

- Spaces with some curved walls or ceiling surfaces seem more beautiful than those that are entirely rectilinear.

Windows are important architectural elements of a space:

- To harvest all the benefits of natural light, skylights can be important additions to spaces where in-wall windows would admit daylight but also an ugly (for example, industrial) view. Clerestory windows (these are relatively small windows close to the top of the wall in a room) can also help move natural light into a space without displaying unattractive views.

- We prefer to have smaller windows in spaces where we want to feel safe, such as in bedrooms and bathrooms; larger windows and skylights work well in living rooms, kitchens, and family rooms.

- We'd rather be in rooms with windows and/or skylights than spaces without windows or skylights.

- Windows make rooms seem less crowded, so they're great in spaces where parties will be thrown, for example.

There are other architectural features that are preferred and make us feel good.

- We relax in spaces that are symmetrical, balanced, rhythmic, and harmonious. When all are present in a space, we can become very, very calm, which not all PlaceTypes enjoy.

- Symmetry in a space makes it seem a more pleasant place to be, as well as slightly more formal. As discussed earlier, there are two primary types of symmetry, reflected and rotated. You can create symmetry by using the same architectural feature (such as a column), color, pattern, image, or type of ornament several times in the same room.

- Balancing is arranging things that seem to have equal visual weight on either side of a pivot point, like the midpoint of a seesaw. Symmetrical balance, like reflective symmetry, signals "formality" in a space. Asymmetrical balance, or balance created by placing objects that appear heavier closer to the balance pivot point, is not quite as relaxing as symmetrical balance and can be tricky to plan. Things that are darker colors seem heavier than those that are lighter colors. Objects that draw our eyes to them either because of their colors compared to other things nearby or because of their shapes, textures, or something else need to be placed closer to that imaginary middle line because they seem heavier to us. For balance, relatively less eye-catching objects which seem lighter, should be farther away from the focal point. Radial balance involves the same sort of repetition as rotated symmetry, but around a central hub, like spokes around the center of a wheel.

- Rhythm is repetition of something—like an arch, a violet color, or pattern in wallpaper, for instance. Repetition is relaxing.

- Having a common theme makes a space harmonious, and harmony makes us feel comfortable and relaxed. The common themes that lead to harmony can take a variety of forms; they can be the use of shades of the same color (e.g., a blue room), or something cultural (such as being Greek), or features that relate to a hobby (think: sailing). If the common theme is too hard to identify, the stabilizing effects of harmony are lost.

Integrating Sensory Experiences

All of the physical experiences we have in a space, even the ones that we don't consciously perceive, combine to produce a single emotional, cognitive, and physical response to it and the objects in it. Effects are also proportional within a single sensory channel. A generally restful color scheme that features a small patch of an energizing color—say a throw pillow—will be relaxing overall, for example.

We prefer that all of our sensory experiences within an area are consistent with each other—that colors that relax us are paired with scents which have the same effect, for example.

For each of us, one sensory channel—vision, hearing, touch, scent, or taste—has the strongest effect on the emotional state in our brain. It's our dominant sense. In a chapter to come, you'll learn how to identify yours.

Space Management

When we were living on the savanna on our way to becoming modern, we could move around to change the light and temperature, relocating from the sun to the shade or the shade to the sun, for example. But today, we don't have as much flexibility to change our location if we're trying to cook our dinner, finish a project, or sleep through the night, so our environment needs to provide us with options; selecting among those options gives us control of our experiences.

Humans live better lives when they feel that they have a comfortable level of control over what's going on around them. They like to have a reasonable amount of influence over how warm a space is, how brightly lit it is, if there's a breeze, and so on. Creating desired sound and scent environments is also good for us psychologically, which helps explain in part why home air fresheners sell so well: they create "smell zones." Control increases our mental comfort and well-being. We're only really comfortable and completely relaxed in a space when we feel we can determine the sorts of experiences we'll have there, and we do our best intellectual work in places where we have control.

People like to feel that they can set light and temperature levels as desired, but too many choices are too much. We're more comfortable in a space with four lighting presets than a rotating lighting control dial that provides hundreds of lighting options.

An important part of feeling in control is having a territory—yes, a territory, like a chipmunk or a raccoon. Territories are just as crucial to human well-being as they are to the well-being of other animals. All humans, once they leave babyhood, need to control a space that is viewed by everyone else as theirs. A territory can be defined by walls and a door, but it may also be established by the edge of a rug, by a change of pattern in that rug, or by a difference in ceiling height or some other physical sign that is clear and difficult to misinterpret.

Groups need territories, too, where they can share their common experiences, ideas, and values. Families, however they are defined, need spaces that are clearly theirs. In suburbia, the proverbial white picket fence distinguishes one family's space from that of the next, and in cities apartment doors do the same thing. In any family, parents are a team and need their own space separate from that of their children. Traditionally, parents' most carefully defined territory has begun at the door of their master bedroom, but home offices are often also the domain of parents.

When we personalize a space, we feel more satisfied with it.

Individuals customize their territories, and groups do, too. Putting out a few baby pictures, draping the afghan that grandma made over the back of the couch, and leaving a pair of slippers by an armchair proclaim your ownership of a space. When we personalize a space, we feel more satisfied with it and really relax. One of the reasons that we can decompress in places we've put our own stamp on is that those places are now sending messages that we wish to hear ourselves and that we want others to recognize. We're proclaiming that we are either good at our job, a philanthropist (or at least concerned enough about the world to volunteer), or an athlete—why else would we have a lamp made from tennis rackets? When we get busy or distracted, the things out for all to see in our home keep us from losing track of what we value about ourselves, and those physical cues are particularly important to our well-being.

Work groups and families need to tell their group stories in the spaces they share. That means a French beret hanging on a picture hook in the family room to recall their trip to Paris, or a ping-pong table for family members that signals their common interest in the sport or in relaxing. Shelves of books can indicate an enthusiasm for reading and ideas.

Getting along with others goes better when we know what's important to them, and we're always reading the messages that others are sending. We're continually trying to understand each other in order to build relationships, or at least keep a conversation going. And we all know this. That's why we get so worked up about selecting the right sofa from all of the equally comfortable options available and consider picture frame options as carefully as our choices for the images inside them. We trust the messages that people send through their stuff more than those that they formally proclaim—it seems harder to lie with things than words.

Do you wonder what messages you need to send with your office or home? Think about the three, four, or five photos that you'd like to have—or already have—that illustrate the professional (for your office) or the personal (for your home) highlights of your life. What's in those photos? Are you pictured an image with your first child just after he or she was born, the moment that made you a parent? Winning a sailing prize? Debating philosophical points with your mom or dad? If so, make sure the stuff in your office or home (photographs, souvenirs, etc.) signals without words that you relish your family, live to sail, or are interested in ideas.

Trying to send a signal that is not true to who you are with the things in your home won't work. First of all, it's incredibly difficult to do well. For us mere mortals, it's inevitable that we slip up when we try to send a message that doesn't mesh with who we think we really are, and inconsistencies are noted by all viewers. Telling a story that isn't yours is also stressful since it's so difficult. Putting out a few meaningful things is important. Clutter makes us tense, but so does a place that seems empty because tabletops and walls are bare. An earlier section of this book talks about clutter and visual complexity.

Control and guests make for a dicey combination. We feel more comfortable when we control what happens in our home, and guests are happiest when they also have some influence over the places where they're sleeping. Visitor control can be more graciously provided when people are sleeping in separate rooms with doors than when they're retiring for the night in the living room, but efforts to transfer some control to guests are desirable in any case. Guests can, for example, perhaps have some influence on the temperature setting on the thermostat and whether windows are open or closed. They should be able to turn off lights near their bed while they're sleeping and determine when they retire for the evening. Guests also must be able to leave out some of their belongings, particularly near where they're sleeping, so they can establish a territory there. You may not like seeing someone else's travel alarm clock in your living room or guests' toiletries in your bathroom. Get over it. If you're the host and all else fails, scent your home with the sorts of smells researchers have found to be relaxing (see the section on smell-scaping your home, which was talked about earlier), play calming music (again, discussed earlier), and grit your teeth until your guests head home.

To keep ourselves in good psychological shape, we need the ability to determine who's around us, both at work and at home, and sometimes the number of other people that any of us want to be able to see and hear is exactly zero. Privacy isn't just for individuals, groups need it too. So both individuals and groups need to be able to be with others (visually and acoustically) or to be separate from them on their own schedule. This is not just for adults; once kids reach the age of three, they need to be able to be with or apart from other people as they choose (and obviously within reason).

People don't have privacy if others can intrude, whether intentionally or unintentionally, on the space where they've tried to isolate themselves. If we can't determine who might wander through our space, a place is not private. Doors generally enable us to have privacy. So do other rules that we've clearly established with the people who live with us, such as being left alone while in the grape arbor at the end of the garden or in the attic window seat—these signals are developed over time by people sharing a space. When we're alone in a private space, we won't be distracted, but just being in a place where we're free of distractions doesn't guarantee we have privacy.

When people, whether alone or in groups, have privacy, they are visually and acoustically separated from others to the extent that they wish to be. When people have territories, they have a space where they can probably expect to have privacy, but for some, the space that's private isn't where their territory is located. For example, part of the family territory may be its backyard, but the neighbors may easily be able to see and hear all that happens there. The space where people have privacy can be a spa-type bathroom, but there may be so many users of that bathroom that no individual family member can claim it as their territory and personalize it.

The reason you have to make sure all the individuals and groups (for example, parents) living in your home will be left alone sometimes is because when we decide to separate ourselves from other people, we do a lot of hard but crucial psychological work. When we're not being seen, heard, or disturbed by others, or vice versa, we make sense of the recent events in our lives and organize our thoughts. This helps us not only move forward with the projects and tasks that are important to us, but also reduces the levels of stress we're experiencing. Being stressed is bad because it uses up mental energy we could be devoting to doing something positive. When people can't help but interfere with other people's attempts to be alone (for example, because they have to walk through a particular room to get to another one they need to be in), it makes both parties uncomfortable.

Being alone needs to be a choice in order for people to gain psychological dividends from it. Being sent to our room solo is a punishment when we're children, with good reason. Humans are social animals who, regardless of their psychological profiles, need at least some time with other people every day or they have difficulty focusing and feel on edge.

Telephone conversations are often meant to be heard only by the people on the phone. Now that people can talk anywhere, anytime, phone calls are often inadvertently public at one or both ends of the line. People talking on the phone on their front porch may unintentionally share information about their finances with their neighbors, for example. Parents on business calls at home can make children concerned about all sorts of things when young minds set out to decipher the half of a telephone conversation they've overheard. The best way to prevent difficult situations from developing is for those using telephones to pay attention to what they're saying and where. Identifying a comfortable but acoustically isolated (really, not just wishful thinking here) "telephone zone" can minimize the likelihood that parts of conversations will be overheard. This sort of telephone base camp can also keep people who are not on the phone from being distracted while they're trying to focus on something they're reading. Old-fashioned phone booths may be something that every modern (especially open-plan) home and office needs. If there will be multiple offices in one house, it's a good idea to put the workspaces at opposite ends of the home, if space allows, so that telephone noise pollution from one office doesn't contaminate the other.

Environmental Cues

We read elements of the physical environment to identify cues in them. Those cues may remind us about how we plan for a space to be used or how our host, the owner of a space, wants us to behave.

Do you prefer that meals be a little more formal? Perhaps you associate formality with peacefulness. Then put a white tablecloth on the table before each meal. We link white tablecloths with more formal dinners and act accordingly.

Blackboards and whiteboards signal "school," so they're useful in-home schoolrooms even if no one ever writes on them. Seeing that board will help students focus on learning. Whiteboards also signal "work," so they can get people in a home office into a productive frame of mind.

Healthy Eating

Researchers have extensively studied how design can encourage us to eat in ways that make us healthier.

- People eat more when they can see where the food is prepared and stored; they travel from the eating area to the food preparation and storage area more frequently and end up consuming more food when they do. If you have an open floor plan that allows people dining to see into kitchen spaces, block this visual connection using screens or something similar if healthy eating is an issue in your home.

- We tend to eat more unhealthy food snacks in spaces that are cluttered and disorganized, so if the goal is homes and workplaces that support healthy eating choices, clutter-busting is not optional.

- Seeing relatively thin sculptures of humans while eating has been tied to healthier eating.

- When light levels are lower, we tend to eat more slowly and ultimately less than when they're brighter. We are, however, more likely to eat healthier foods when we're in more brightly lit spaces. We also tend to linger longer over meals when spaces have relatively dimmer and warmer light as opposed to relatively brighter and cooler light. While we're lingering, there's the possibility that we'll decide to eat second helpings of food or dessert.

- Relaxing colors, those that are not very saturated but are relatively bright, such as a light sage green, are the best shades to feature in spaces where you want to eat responsibly. Looking at more energizing colors can encourage faster eating and consuming more food. Warm colors tend to amplify our appetites.

- People are calmer and more mindful of what they're eating in spaces that are relatively quiet, say with sound volumes of fifty-five dB versus seventy dB. This is about the volume of most casual conversations and is the volume set on most televisions.

- Solid fronted cabinets, instead of ones with glass fronts, make it harder to see food inside and be tempted by it.

- Using floral air fresheners in kitchens as opposed to ones that smell like food (cinnamon, for example) can discourage snacking and other unhealthy eating.

- Seating areas and televisions in kitchens may encourage people to linger in kitchens, close to all sorts of food that they probably shouldn't eat, so finding a place to hang out that's farther away from the kitchen is probably good for your heart and your waistline.

- If possible, try to enter your home via a door that doesn't open into your kitchen, since people who enter their homes through doors into their kitchens tend to have less healthy diets.

Designing for Sleep

Design that helps people fall asleep more quickly and sleep better once they're asleep has been thoroughly researched. The need to avoid screens close to bedtime that emit lots of cool blue light, such as iPads in their standard mode, has been frequently discussed in the popular press, but there's more to making a space "sleep friendly" than setting the screens of electronics to a warmer type of nighttime illumination.

- You should make the space you'll sleep in as dark as possible. Use blackout curtains if necessary to make your sleeping area dark. Sleeping in dark spaces is good for your mental and physical health.

- As discussed earlier, lighting that is warmer and dimmer is more relaxing, so it's best in places where people plan to sleep.

- Sound volumes in sleep areas should be less than thirty-five to forty dB, which is the same volume as a library or a peaceful rural space. When sound levels are higher, sleepers have higher blood pressure readings. Installing sound dampening insulation can cut bedroom sound levels.

- Lavender and other relaxing or anxiety reducing scents noted earlier in this book can be good choices for sleeping areas.

- People sleep best in places where the temperature is around sixty-five degrees.

- We like to have privacy while we sleep, so curtains are needed except in unusual circumstances like very rural locations or unusual designs which ensure that people nearby won't be able to see into a bedroom. Also, windows that are higher on walls than usual, which are known as clerestory windows, can block views into sleeping spaces without restricting the amount of natural light in an area.

Living with Living Things

Living with living things—plants and pets—is great for our both our hearts and our heads.

PETS

Designing for happy pets—we'll focus on dogs and cats—is geared to creating spaces where they feel sheltered and where they have just the right level of sensory stimulation. Pets give their owners a great psychological boost, so the time required to pet-proof a house or a workplace, which is a lot like child-proofing one, is time well spent.

- Dogs and cats are happiest when they have a view outside. Smaller pets may be able to jump up and sit on windowsills, but for larger or older ones, only a window that reaches to the floor will provide a view. Wider sills (and also, mainly for cats, wider railings around balconies) make it more comfortable for pets to take a snooze in the sun.

- Dogs and cats, like people, are likely to be in a better mood when they have choices about what to do. So areas where they're kept should allow them to sit in the sun or not, or play or not, or hide or not, and so on, as they choose.

- Some pets are frightened by open stairways, and pets, just like people, can also lose their footing on slippery surfaces.

- Plants pets might be able to chew on must be nontoxic to them.

- Outdoors, pets need access to a mix of surfaces: more permeable ones (such as lawns) to sit on during warmer days and paved surfaces that will hold the heat during cooler months. Also, animals outside need to be able to find shelter both from the sun and inclement weather.

- If there's sufficient sound insulation between homes or offices, dogs will not hear other dogs in these areas, and any barking they might choose to do will be muted.

- Dogs need to be in spaces that are moderately complex visually, just as humans do. In barren spaces, they wilt and become inactive, but when they are in areas with furnishings and things to play with, they can blossom.

- Spaces for cats need built-in opportunities for cats to climb and be high off the ground. Cats will climb whether you plan for it or not, so consciously anticipating their drive to move upward can make life easier on everyone.

- Cats' litter boxes, whether built in or otherwise, should not be located near where the cats eat.

- Seeing an aquarium is calming and improves our mood and mental performance. Having a mix of a few types of fish amplifies the benefits of fish tanks, but a mix is not required to produce these benefits.

PLANTS

When people are around green leafy plants, their lives are much better. Green leafy plants (ideally with rounded leaves) can improve a place by processing the carbon dioxide present, which is important, but they do even more to enhance what's going on in people's minds.

- When we're around a plant or two, our stress levels decline, we feel more confident, and our mood improves. Also, our cognitive performance improves and we're better at problem-solving and concentrating. Being around green indoor plants has been directly linked to enhanced creative thinking.

- Plants nearby increase our feelings of well-being, even in spaces that already have a view of nature.

- When we're in a place with plants, we're also friendlier than we are when plants are absent—so a few plants in a workplace or a family room go a long way towards making the interpersonal atmosphere more pleasant.

- Plants at the back of classrooms, out of students' view, have been found to improve students' comfort, their friendliness to other students, and their behavior during class, so plants are an important addition to any homeschooling areas.

- And plants don't have to actually be real to provide these benefits (except for the carbon dioxide processing). A realistic artificial plant—which you know when you see it because you don't realize it's actually artificial—does the same good things for what's happening inside our brains that live plants do. Artificial plants can, for example, improve well-being and increase the likelihood of positively interacting with others.

- Live plants do have particular scents, and smelling some of them has been linked to desirable outcomes such as better memory performance, as discussed earlier. Plants selected can support productive scent-scaping of an area.

- Too many plants in a space makes us tense; they make our environment too complex visually. A single plant that is six inches to a foot tall can be a great addition to a space. Having a couple of plants in view at any time is sufficient for all sorts of good things to happen in our heads. More make a space too complex.

Men and Women

There are some differences in how men and women experience the worlds around them. Knowing about these differences makes it easier to design spaces that will be shared by people of both genders and can sometimes be useful in settling arguments between people of different genders.

- Men and women seem to process colors in different ways, and those differences have repercussions for the design of spaces to be used by either men or women. Knowing about these differences also makes it easier to understand disagreements between male and female couples about what colors should be used in any part of a home. Blue is the most common favorite color of both men and women across the planet, but women, regardless of culture, generally prefer redder colors than men. This means, for example, that the blues women covet are redder (think violet). Women are better able to distinguish differences in red-orange type colors than men are. When colors are used in combination, which is most of the time, women are more likely than men to prefer that mixed colors be light or not very saturated. Women also are more emotionally responsive to changes in the saturation and brightness of colors than men.

- Men are more sensitive to fine details and rapid movement in what they see, and women are generally better at distinguishing various colors.

- Women are better at noticing differences in visual textures than men.

- Women generally have a more acute sense of touch than men. Because their fingertips are generally smaller, the sensory receptors on female fingers are more tightly packed than those on men's fingers. This difference has repercussions for things such as responses to materials; for example, women may experience two textures as different that men feel are the same.

- Women have better senses of smell than men. They are more apt to notice if a scent is present and are also better at identifying particular smells.

- Women generally prefer temperatures that are a couple of degrees warmer than men do, so women prefer a place to be 23 to 24 degrees Centigrade, or 74 to 75 degrees Fahrenheit, while men find it comfortable to be in a space that is 20 to 21 degrees Centigrade, or 68 to 69 degrees Fahrenheit. Some of these differences may be due to clothing worn by each sex.

- Men and women generally choose to sit in different ways, which has implications for furniture selections in homes and offices. Men prefer to "open up" and "spread out" while sitting, while women generally sit with their limbs closer to their bodies.

- Women often maintain larger personal space zones than men, regardless of culture. Women are particularly uncomfortable when they're farther from someone than they'd like to be, while the reverse is true for men, who are more highly stressed by being closer to another person than they'd prefer. All these differences in personal spacing make good arguments for having furniture in homes and workplaces that is easily moved or that has extra wide seats so that people can scoot over and be a little closer or scoot back and be a little farther from whomever they are speaking with.

- Things that are slimmer, shinier, rounder, curvier, in lighter colors, and that have more colors are perceived to be feminine, while those that are bulkier, in darker colors, matte finish, angular, and have fewer colors and straighter lines seem more masculine.

- When people who aren't architects are asked to design homes, the homes designed by women have more shared spaces and curved walls and fewer square feet than those designed by men.

National Culture and Design

You can move away from the place where you were born, but you won't leave behind what you learned when you were little about how to use design to support ideas and activities. Do you think that these differences can't be too important? Think again.

You've learned the design-related rules of your own culture very well, but you won't always be with people who were raised in the same country that you were. The variety of ways that people from diverse national cultures can perceive design issues can lead to disagreements when you marry someone from a different part of the world, for example. The material included in this section can't comprehensively address all issues that may arise, but it can give you some clues as to worldwide variations in place experiences. The different associations various cultures have to colors were discussed earlier in this chapter.

Trouble can start when people grow up speaking different languages. Some languages clearly differentiate between male and female nouns. Remember when you took French in high school and "the" was translated as "le" with masculine nouns and "la" with feminine nouns? French distinguishes male and female nouns. People whose first language has gendered nouns, such as French and Spanish, still retain impressions derived from the gendered nouns of their primary language even when speaking other languages (like English) that don't assign gender to nouns at all. As an example, the researchers who uncovered this link studied nouns such as "bridge," which are masculine in some European languages and feminine in others. People who first learned languages in which "bridge" is masculine described bridges as being sturdy and strong. Those who grew up speaking languages in which "bridge" is feminine described bridges as more elegant and beautiful.

Culture seems to influence the processes through which we gather information from the world around us. Research has shown that people raised in different parts of the world literally don't even see the same things when they look at a place or an image. For example, people reared in the West are much more attuned to the focal (or main) visual element in a scene, while people raised in the Far East are more apt to pay attention to a whole scene. So people raised in the West touring a model apartment will be focused on the refrigerator or stove in the kitchen, while, in the same kitchen, those raised in the far East will initially take in the whole scene, but if quizzed later, will not recall as many details about the same appliances. They will however likely be able to report details about backsplashes and flooring that people reared in the West would not have noticed.

Generational Differences

Worried about how the information in this chapter needs to be modified for different generations of people who will use a space? Don't be. For example, each generation's response to color, saturation, and brightness is the same.

Generational differences in the ability to multitask and focus amidst distractions are often discussed, particularly when offices are being designed. Human minds evolve slowly, however, at geologic speed, and for now and for all the time that any of us will be alive or that structures built today will stand, people from any working generation doing focused thinking in an office will need to be in the same sort of place.

There are some life stage differences, mainly related to how our sensory apparatus works and the state of our brains, that influence how people prefer to use space or optimally should experience it. These are discussed later in this book. For example, older eyes can have difficulty picking out contrasts between colors, and young people's minds develop in very particular ways that influence how they analyze their environments. Other life stage differences relate more to objects in place than to their preferred design. For example, people with young children will need baby gates to prevent their children from toppling down stairs, but those parents will select baby gates whose design meshes with the parents' PlaceTypes.

Putting It All Together

All of our physical experiences in a space together influence how we ultimately think and behave and our overall stimulation level. Our optimal stimulation level varies from situation to situation, and sensory experiences need to be coordinated accordingly. When we're doing something that requires mental focus or concentration, our environment should be generally more relaxing, and when we're up to something that doesn't require so much focus, maybe because we've done it many times before or because it is less mentally challenging, a more energizing environment is best. When you're doing knowledge work that requires your full mental effort, say coming up with a new advertising slogan or doing a complex financial analysis, a less energizing environment is best, but when you're answering routine emails, a more energizing space is better. These differences in optimal stimulation levels make it handy to have several places to work. How relatively stimulating or relaxing an experience is has frequently been mentioned in earlier sections of this book.

Do you find yourself confused about whether what you're doing is mentally demanding or not? It can be challenging if you think that the ideal place for your work it is a quiet, low-key space such as a cabin in the woods (but with plumbing and air-conditioning). If you could successfully do whatever you're up to at the airport while you sit, waiting for a flight in a crowd of people, then it's not very challenging for you.

Some areas in your home should definitely be relaxing; for example, the space where you sleep should help you drift off into dreamland—it shouldn't be energizing at all. Other spaces such as living rooms will have higher or lower desired energy levels depending on PlaceType, and the optimal design of those areas will vary accordingly.

People categorize many places they've been as special, and they create their own personal place-myths. The spot on Fifth Avenue in New York City where they were standing with their partner at the moment when they decided to marry is burned into their place memory bank, and the colors, patterns, scents, textures, and sounds they remember from that experience will evoke positive moods, as will the beach cottage where they spent many blissful summer afternoons connecting with their grandparents, and perhaps the university library carrel where their life plan crystallized—or fell apart. These place experiences are the context within which future spaces are assessed and experienced. These experiences influence if we will be happy, healthy, and wealthy—in body and spirit—in a future space with similar attributes.

Place memories are multisensory. Our memory bank of place histories evolves over time as more experiences are added; it can never be ignored. If the walls in your mean uncle's living room were a rich butterscotch, you will never happily paint a room in your home that color.

You should use the associations you've developed to particular sensory experiences—colors, scents, textures, sounds, etc.—to guide your future design decisions. The options presented in this book do not require you to choose a particular color for the walls of your bedroom, nor a specific pattern for the upholstery on your living room couch or a certain faucet in your bathroom, to support your life and PlaceType. Options are always presented in ways that indicate your options. For example, if a pattern of a certain visual complexity is suggested for upholstery, you'll have many options to choose from—you can find one that meets your design objectives but that doesn't look at all like the botanical print you associate with your unpleasant Aunt Joan, yet does remind you of clouds floating overhead on a bright spring day.

Home and Office Tour!

We'll be traveling through homes and offices in the rest of this book, and the question that will guide our journey through them is: What is "success" in this space?

Would it be:

- Relaxing alone or meditating

- Relaxing with other people

- Feeling mentally or physically invigorated all by yourself

- Feeling mentally or physically invigorated with a group of people

- Thinking great thoughts all by yourself

- Thinking great thoughts with other people

Room labels are great, but it's more important to design for what you'll do in a space than for what an area's official label is. Think about the functionality for specific space types noted and focus on those, not on the room names. Most of us want our guests to relax in our living room, but maybe you don't. If you don't, instead of following the recommendations for living room design, apply those from the space type that more accurately reflects the atmosphere you'd like to encourage in an area.

Generally, the sorts of moods and activities that are desired in various areas of homes and offices are:

- Kitchen: Relaxed eating and food production (cooking)

- Dining room: Eating, either alone or with others, while relaxed

- Living room: Socializing with others (most likely not family); a relatively more formal, positive mood and moderate to relaxed energy level

- Family room [in some cases the same as the living room]: Socializing (most likely with family), relatively less formal, positive mood and moderate to relaxed energy level

- Office, home or elsewhere: Positive mood, cognitively productive energy level, ability to concentrate and work productively with others

- Laundry or exercise room: Positive mood, high energy, relatively physical (not cognitive) tasks supported

- Storage areas: Either positive or negative mood acceptable, variable energy levels as needed to support task accomplishment

- Bathroom: Low or high energy level desired depending on person and situation (but lower, deeply relaxing energy level generally preferred), positive mood supported

If an area in your home or workplace needs to have multiple purposes, consider each of those purposes as you begin the design process. It often works well to design a dual function space so that while engaging in one activity, you can't see the space that's best for the other. Imagine a bedroom in which you will also set up your home office. You'll sleep better if you can't see your desk as you lie in bed, and you'll work more effectively if you can't see your bed as you work.

Read on, because all your world's a stage, and you need to have the right sets.

CHAPTER 3

WHO YOU ARE

Your personality is your approach to living your life. It affects whether you are more likely to spend a Saturday morning drinking coffee with a few friends at a spot you discovered years ago or energetically bopping from the dry cleaners to the hardware store to the grocery store, checking an item off your to-do list at each stop. It determines the sort of job that works best for you and which life partner will make you the happiest.

Personality also should drive the design of spaces where you will be happy, healthy, wealthy (at least in spirit), and wise. Decades of research on personality and design—and years of practical experience—make that very clear.

Our personalities have repercussions for how we should live in the physical world because they have a fundamental influence on how we want to experience life.

Humans are wonderfully complex creatures, and many factors combine to create our overall personalities. Rigorous scientific research has shown that a few of them are particularly important to consider as design decisions are made. Each of us needs to sleep, eat, hang out with others (who we choose, when we choose), and get all sorts of work done during each day, for starters. Elements of our personalities determine how furniture should be designed and placed when we're doing each of these things, the best patterns to use in upholstery and rugs, and where walls should be (and if there should even be walls). Design-relevant factors that reflect how a person should live in the physical world determine someone's PlaceType.

To learn more about your personality and how to support it with the design of the world around you, select the word or phrase in the following sentences that you think best reflects who you are most of the time.

I am an **outgoing/reserved** person

      A   B

I am **more comfortable with a plan/more easygoing.**

      C   D

I **love to try new things/like to stick with the tried-and-true.**

      E   F

The first dimension of personality we need to learn more about is whether you're relatively more energized by the world outside yourself, and therefore relatively more extraverted, or by your internal world, so relatively more introverted. The second dimension of personality related to PlaceType is conscientiousness, which, in short, is how engaged (relatively more conscientious) or laid back (relatively less conscientious) you are. The third dimension is openness to experiences. People who are relatively more open to experience are more daring, while those who are relatively less to experience are more practical. Compare your three answers (and their corresponding letters) to the chart below:

If you're categorized as…	Your PlaceType is:
A, C, and E	Adventurer
A, C, and F	Guardian
A, D, and E	Maverick
A, D, and F	Dynamo

B, C, and E	Investigator
B, C, and F	Sage
B, D, and E	Maestro
B, D, and F	Maven

Good design follows when you know about your own PlaceType as well as the PlaceTypes of the other people who will use a space. For most of the next few chapters, I will talk in terms of an individual user of a space, but later on, I will discuss how people with different PlaceTypes can happily share a home. You can use this quiz to identify the personality traits of people with whom you share a space by anticipating how they should answer each of the questions posed. Developing a space that meshes with your PlaceType is not always easy, but each change you make in your home to support your PlaceType makes living there a better experience.

We settle into our adult personalities around the age of twenty-five, and personality tests work best for people twenty-five and older. You may see consistencies between the personalities of children sharing a home with you and the adult personality dimensions we talk about in depth, however.

As you read through the PlaceType write-ups below, you'll see how those A or a B, C or D, E or F qualities influence the sort of place in which you are most likely to live your best life. Consider your living room. Knowing about your PlaceType will guide your answers to questions such as: What should the line of the furniture be like—more rectilinear or curvier? How about the patterns in the upholstery and wallpaper? What sort of art should be added to the space? The PlaceType system answers these questions and many others.

The PlaceTypes can be organized into four groups:

- Enthusiasts: Adventurers and Guardians thrive in more energetic and coordinated spaces that continually evolve to meet their changing needs. Guardians prefer more historic, time-honored elements around them than Adventurers do. Adventurers are relatively more extraverted, conscientious, and open to experiences, while Guardians are relatively more extraverted, and conscientious, and less open to experience.

- Intellectuals: Investigators and Sages live their best lives in places where the vibe is calm, understated, and contemplative. Investigators prosper among the more daring, while Sages flourish with the mainstream. Investigators are relatively more introverted, conscientious, and open to experiences. Sages are relatively more introverted and conscientious and less open to experience.

- Catalysts: Mavericks and Dynamos do well in spaces that are lush and nurture relationships with other people. Mavericks are more comfortable with alternative design than Dynamos. Mavericks are more extraverted and open to experience and less conscientious. Dynamos are more extraverted and less conscientious and open to experience.

- Wizards: Maestros and Mavens succeed in places where the design is edited to a soothing, sublime perfection. Maestros relish stylish options that Mavens don't. Maestros are more introverted and open to experience and less conscientious. Mavens are more introverted and less conscientious and open to experience.

It's a good idea to read all of the PlaceType sections that follow. Learning about other PlaceTypes will help you better understand both your own type and how to design places you'll share with people with other PlaceTypes, which is the focus of Chapter 9.

Each of us has a dominant sense as well as a PlaceType. Our dominant sense is the most direct route to our emotional core. In the Western world, many people's dominant sense is vision, but any sense can be dominant in one person or another. If your dominant sense is smell, you have an even deeper connection to particular smells associated with pleasant (and unpleasant) events in your life than the rest of us. You are also more likely to remember smells associated with important events in your life than others are. The same sorts of links are found in people whose dominant sense is vision or touch or hearing or taste.

How can you tell what your dominant sense is? Think about the single happiest event of your life: it might be your wedding, your graduation, or meeting your first child or puppy. What sensory experience comes to mind first for that event? That "first sense" is your dominant sense. Do you remember the smell of your new baby or something about how your new baby looked? Is your first sensory memory of the feel of their skin or the sound of their breathing? Another approach to identifying your dominant sense is to imagine going on a dream trip—what pops into your mind first? Which sense is involved? For example, if you think about a beach vacation, do you notice the feel of the sun on your skin? If so, touch is your dominant sense.

Now that you know your PlaceType, you're ready to read the next chapter to learn more about how it should affect your design decisions.

CHAPTER 4

THE PLACETYPE SYSTEM

When design is consistent with the PlaceTypes of the people who will use a place, it enhances well-being, making positive life experiences more likely. The PlaceType system eliminates a lot of costly trial and error (both in terms of time and/or money) from the office or home design process.

Extraversion/Introversion and Design

The personality test you took in Chapter 3 indicates whether you are relatively more extraverted or relatively more introverted. Your level of extraversion and introversion matters because:

- People who are relatively more extraverted are energized by the world around them, while those who are relatively more introverted get the same sort of charge from their own thoughts. Both people who are relatively more extraverted and more introverted are equally socially adept, and both can get along well with others. People who are relatively more introverted are not shy or social outcasts by any means. Having other people around ups the energy levels of all people, but extraverts are more likely to find this higher energy level desirable than introverts.

- A primary difference between people who differ on their levels of extraversion and introversion is that extraverts prefer lusher environments, while introverts prefer more carefully curated spaces. So, people who are relatively more extraverted enjoy richer sensory environments, ones where sights, scents, sounds, and textures contribute to a rich physical experience. Introverts prefer a carefully developed set of experiences that combine to create a more restrained space. People who are relatively more extraverted prefer more saturated colors than people who are relatively more introverted, for example. People who are relatively more introverted are relatively more effective processors of sensory stimuli than people who are relatively more extraverted, so they are more likely to notice scents, for example.

- The cognitive performance of people doing knowledge-work-type thinking who are relatively more introverted is more negatively affected by distractions at work—for example, nearby conversations—than the performance of relatively more extraverted people in the same situation.

- Individuals who are relatively more extraverted do their best at whatever they're trying to accomplish (for example, knowledge work) in a space that's a little more energizing, while introverts will do the same task or activity well in spaces that are less energizing. In Chapter 2, we covered the basics of making a space energizing or relaxing.

- Multi-person seats (for example, sofas) are more popular with people who are more extraverted than they are with people who are more introverted. Introverts are bigger fans of single-person chairs than extraverts.

- People who are more extraverted prefer smaller personal spaces than people who are more introverted do.

- Relatively more seats should be included in areas to be used by more extraverted people and relatively fewer in areas used by more introverted ones.

- Higher levels of extraversion have been linked to a more favorable response to open furniture arrangements. Open furniture arrangements don't have physical barriers such as desks between people speaking.

- People who are relatively more extraverted have a more positive response to open-plan floor plans than people who are relatively more introverted. People who are relatively more introverted prefer more interior walls and more clearly segmented spaces in homes.

- People who are relatively more introverted prefer art showing nature scenes, while people who are relatively more extraverted have more positive opinions about art that depicts people.

- Since people who are relatively more introverted can more easily become over-energized by being around other people than extraverts, it is particularly important that people who are relatively more introverted have something in the environment to which they can "gracefully" divert their eyes when being around others is getting to be too much. This is technically known as a "focal element." "Gracefully" in this case means without seeming to be rude. Some examples of focal points that people who are relatively more introverted could look at without being rude are fish tanks, windows, or pieces of art located in the triangular area in front of them to which their eyes can travel without needing to pivot one's head.

- People who are relatively more extraverted are more comfortable communicating information about themselves than people who are relatively more introverted. This means that in an office, they're happier personalizing their workplace with a souvenir of their last vacation than someone who is relatively more introverted.

Conscientiousness and Design

People can be more or less conscientious. People who are more conscientious have a different approach to life than people who are less conscientious, but neither way of thinking is any better or any worse than the other. The main difference between the two is that people who are more conscientious are relatively more engaged and focused, particularly on work-type goals, than people who are less conscientious. People who are less conscientious are more laid-back. People who are more conscientious seem more self-disciplined and have a greater respect for duty. People who are conscientious are also more driven to achieve, however they define achievement, than people who are relatively less conscientious. The more conscientious among us are more likely to be organized than those of us who are less conscientious.

- People who are more conscientious are more interested in efficient, effective performance than people who are less conscientious. Environmental design that enhances performance takes many forms, including making sure that a space is brightly lit; in the hands of people without a lot of training in lighting, efforts to accomplish this can result in overlighting. More angular design elements have been tied to efficiency.

- People who more actively direct their own lives, for example, continually work with the world around themselves to make it fit their needs at that moment—they'll spend time rearranging furniture and repurposing rooms that others won't. Since this rearranging and repurposing will go on whether it can be accomplished easily or not, acknowledging the potential for future changes during the design process keeps spaces from "uglying up" as changes are made.

- People who are more or less conscientious have different approaches to orderliness. Those who are relatively more conscientious adore it and want their environment to support it, while people who are less conscientious are not as strongly motivated to be orderly, although positive experiences in the modern world require at least moderate levels of organization. Organizational tools provided for people who are relatively more conscientious can be relatively less obvious, as people who are more conscientious will seek them out. Organizational and efficiency type aids in the offices and homes of people who are relatively less conscientious need to be much less subtle and much more obvious, so that they can't be ignored. People who are relatively more conscientious will also have a natural proclivity to keep clutter in check that is missing from people who are relatively less conscientious. People who are relatively more conscientious are likely to prize visual symmetry more than people who are less conscientious.

- Individuals who are relatively more conscientious are also more concerned about cleanliness than those who are less conscientious. This means that their homes and workplaces should not only be designed to be relatively straightforward to clean but also less likely to look dirty in the first place.

- People who are more conscientious are more likely to have a sense of duty about things such as preserving heirlooms than people who are less conscientious.

Openness to Experience and Design

People who are more open to experience prize creativity and intellectual stimulation to a greater extent than people who are less open to experience. Those who are relatively more open to experience are more attuned to the new, different, and daring, while people who are relatively less open to experience have more respect for the tried and true and are apt to be more practical. Different than the norm can be good or bad. We can bring unusual things into our offices and homes, or we can use more typical objects in unusual ways. People may decide to add a distinctive African drum to the décor in their living room, and they can also decide that drum should function as an end table, or, with some modifications, as a planter. Some people have what is known as a high "need for uniqueness;" they value things that are different just because they are different, but people who are open to experience do not necessarily have a high need for uniqueness.

- While people who are relatively more conscientious will decide to change their home or workplace as their professional or personal needs change, people with relatively more openness to experience are more likely to change their homes to reflect new ideas and things they are exposed to.

- People who are relatively more open to experience are more receptive to design solutions—as well as situations—that are novel or unusual; they are receptive to being unconventional and nontraditional, while people who are relatively less open to experience have the opposite design preferences. People who are relatively more open to experience are also more interested in aesthetics and the arts generally than people who are relatively less open to experience.

- Individuals who are relatively more open to experience have a more positive orientation to a variety of experiences than people who are relatively less open to experiences.

- People who are more open to experience have a wider range of interests than people who are less open to experience, which is often reflected in the wide variety of subjects covered in the books on their bookshelves or iPad.

- People who are more open to experience may have more unconventional hobbies, such as breeding new strains of orchids, that need to be supported by a home environment than people who are less open to experience.

- People who are more open to experience need to remember that some of the customizations they may build into their homes, to support hobbies, for example, can be difficult to undo and may pose sales challenges if they decide to move. This is particularly important because people who are more open to experience are more likely to move than other people. So, taking a longer term perspective, people who are relatively more open to experience may find it useful to customize their homes with an eye to recreating a desired ambiance or capability in a future home. For example, instead of building in an extensive system of woodworking benches, someone with more openness to experience may decide to create a sectional system of work surfaces on wheels that is easier to move to a new home.

Integrating the design consequences of extraversion/introversion, conscientiousness, and openness to experience results in the development of offices and homes that have positive effects on user well-being. The next few chapters lay out how design can support personality.

CHAPTER 5

ADVENTURERS AND GUARDIANS—SPACES FOR ENTHUSIASTS

Design that makes Enthusiasts feel good radiates confidence, just as Enthusiasts do. Enthusiasts are leaders who enjoy the people and places that support their spirited outlook on life.

- Adventurers and Guardians thrive in powerful spaces with clear points of view that can evolve long-term to meet changing needs—today's dining room may be tomorrow's artist's studio or homeschooling classroom. Built-ins are out and wheels are in with this crew.

- Both Adventurers and Guardians prefer spaces that are complex and intense, with layered sensory experiences, as detailed in the next few pages.

- People who are Enthusiasts like to take control of their physical environments. They do best in spaces that can continually evolve to meet their changing needs. The temperatures, lights, sounds, music, and scents they select as the backdrops for their lives are important to Enthusiasts; they're not "set it once and forget it" types.

- These PlaceTypes are happiest with open environments that enable people in different parts of an office or home to be in constant contact. If you are an Enthusiast, your first step when moving into a new home should be to open up the spaces between your kitchen, dining room, living room, kitchen, and other nearby areas as much as possible. If knocking down walls doesn't make sense for financial or structural reasons, these areas need a unified look and feel.

- Enthusiasts need to make sure that their spaces are easy to keep orderly and well organized. Places to store possessions need doors and drawer fronts that prevent people from seeing their contents.

- Straight lines and rectangular forms should outnumber curving ones in Enthusiasts' homes—Mission style furniture (which features straight horizontal and vertical lines) is a better choice for these PlaceTypes than Chippendale type pieces (which have lots of curves). Geometric wallpapers and carpets should be used instead of florals. No space should just have straight lines or curvy ones in it, but we're talking relative amounts here. So even in an Enthusiast's home, a curvy vase is fine with that geometric wallpaper and mission style furniture. Fireplaces in Enthusiasts' homes should feature straight lines, squares, and rectangles in their panels and moldings; in Adventurer's homes, their design can be more unconventional and in Guardian's homes more traditional.

- Enthusiasts can create places that they enjoy that overpower others. Spaces that would be too stimulating for Investigators, Sages, Maestros, and Mavens can be popular with Enthusiasts. When Enthusiasts are putting together spaces for guests to stay the night, they need to make sure that those guest spaces are places where any visitor, regardless of PlaceType, can actually relax. This can mean fewer added scents and less energizing colors than Enthusiasts usually select. Consciously developing guest spaces with other PlaceTypes in mind means that all guests will be able to relax during their visits to Enthusiasts.

Adventurers

MEET AN ADVENTURER

Ann is an Adventurer. Her happy everyday space is filled with experiences and energy. There are certain things about Ann's personality that we need to keep in mind as we help her create a space that syncs with her PlaceType. First, Ann doesn't let life just happen to her or the places that she lives. She's always working to enhance all her worlds: physical, virtual, social, and cultural. People ask her all the time where she gets her energy, but it's all-natural, except for a few cups of coffee here and there.

One of the reasons for Ann's drive and pep is that she's intellectually very curious, and a score of topics interest her intensely. That's partly why she loves to travel—anywhere—and doesn't hesitate to talk to people when she gets where she's going.

Ann's always interested in what's new to eat, to wear, or for her home. She doesn't necessarily need to own what's new, but she always considers it carefully. There's a lot more to Ann, or any Adventurer, than what's covered in these paragraphs, but all of the things mentioned here are important to consider as we work through how Ann should design her world.

Adventurers' homes can feature multiple intense sensory experiences. Adventurers value unique and vigorous spaces. They live ready to jump spontaneously into whatever seems best, whether that's painting an abstract mural on the living room wall, having a dozen people over for a barbeque, or who knows what else.

Ann needs to use an assortment of several bold smells and rich textures in her home, for example. Hers is the most entrepreneurial of the PlaceTypes from a sensory perspective—always checking out new ways to combine experiences.

BEFORE YOU EVEN GET INSIDE

The home or office experience starts before anyone actually gets to the door of their office or house—it begins with the neighborhood in which it is located. Each PlaceType does its best living in certain sorts of areas. Adventurers should live in zones where there are lots of things that they find interesting going on and where there are apt to be people out and about. These sorts of neighborhoods are easiest to find in cities, though they are scattered throughout suburbs, as well. Satisfying spaces might be filled with restaurants, bookstores, or parks where people run, work out, or do something else. The specific neighborhood should be chosen depending on the Adventurer's particular interests and hobbies.

Since Ann's home is in the right sort of neighborhood, she feels comfortably energized as she walks to her building from the train or her car. Ann lives in the midst of an area packed with ethnic restaurants that she enjoys visiting and tiny independent stores which often have objects in their windows that intrigue her and draw her in to take a look— whether those displays are of Burmese cleaning products, Swedish chocolates, or Amish woodworking tools.

It would be best if the windows in Ann's living room, dining room, and kitchen—nearly every room—faced a space where people can be seen out and about. It's also important for there to be at least some nature in view through those windows; for example, a few trees or a working fountain. People visible from Ann's bedroom might keep her awake at night, but a nature view from her bed will sooth Ann into blissful afternoon naps.

Ann can't change anything about her front door—the condominium board is pretty strict about that—but front doors can be a great way for Adventurers and other PlaceTypes to signal who they are to visitors. In the case of Adventurers, an ideal doorknocker would be intricate in design, produce an unusual but easy to hear sound, and ideally, be the only one of its kind in the world.

No one relishes a front porch on a home more than an Adventurer. If you're an Adventurer and your house will actually be a condo or apartment in a multi-person dwelling, find one with a lobby where people linger.

LIVING ROOMS/FAMILY ROOMS FOR ADVENTURERS

No matter how small or convoluted the entrance to their office or home is, Adventurers need to immediately signal who they are and what's important to them with photographs, wall hangings, objects, and furnishings. This communication is also particularly vital in Guardian, Maverick, and Dynamo homes and offices.

Adventurers make heavy use of their living and family rooms, so it's really important that these spaces support them psychologically. The design of workspaces (not offices!) such as laundry rooms or storage areas, however, don't have as much influence on their well-being, as long as all the equipment in them is functioning well.

Guardians, Mavericks, and Dynamos, like Adventurers, prefer open-plan environments. Living rooms, dining rooms, kitchens, and family rooms all in one space really work for you if you're one of these PlaceTypes.

If an open plan won't or can't happen, try to make sure the main gathering space in an Adventurer's home (probably a living room or family room) is the largest room there. Repurpose spaces if necessary to make the primary social space the largest room in the home; for example, sometimes older homes have bigger dining rooms than living rooms, and the furnishings in these two spaces can be switched.

Light colors on the walls make rooms appear larger, while darker colors make them seem smaller. Since Adventurers want to create an open-plan effect, light colors are in order for their walls—say different versions of the palest greens or the palest blues that you can recognize as green or blue, the naturals mentioned in Chapter 2. One way that you (if you're an Adventurer) and Ann can make a chopped-up space seem more united is to paint all the walls of the rooms you want to "bring together" the same color or, if you must have some variety, nearly identical shades of a single color.

There are other things you can do to feel more comfortable if you're an Adventurer and your living room is not part of an open-plan space. You should arrange furniture so that people sitting in at least a few living room seats have the longest views (or "sightlines") possible through the home. Group some seats so that you can see out the doorways of the rooms where those seats are located and into as many other rooms as possible. It's great if those views through other rooms end with a peek outside.

Spaces will also seem more open if the ceilings seem higher—you can use paint to optically bump up ceilings, as discussed in Chapter 2. Walls also seem higher when moldings at the ceiling are painted the same color as the walls below them.

Even though seemingly high ceilings can be a good thing, having overly tall ceilings isn't necessarily desirable. In homes, make sure the spaces where people will gather don't have ceilings much above ten feet high. A much taller ceiling can make those spaces feel too formal for any socializing hosted by Adventurers. If your primary space for getting together with others has a ceiling a lot over ten feet tall and you're an Adventurer, drop the ceiling a bit over some of the seats. This can be done by actually putting in a lower ceiling or by adding a canopy or something similar over chairs.

Colors that are saturated and darker, such as emerald greens and pumpkin oranges (jewel tones), are the most energizing available, and since you (if you're an Adventurer) enjoy spaces with gusto, select those sorts of colors for use in upholstery and accessories in your home. The highest-energy combinations, the ones Adventurers relish, are those that are across from each other on the color wheel, so you'll want to use some of those—pair reds with greens, oranges with blues, or yellows with purples on throw pillows, etc.

One of the patterns in an Adventurer's living room—on rugs, wallpaper, upholstery, or somewhere else—can have a few curvy design elements in it, but otherwise, curved lines should be hard to find in an Adventurer's living room.

Hardwood floors are an environmental psychology wonder drug, and they are certainly linear, but left uncovered, they are just too austere to satisfy Adventurers—so add area rugs to your living room.

The furniture in an Adventurer's living room should be arranged in very particular ways. First, if you're an Adventurer, you want to look directly at the people with whom you're socializing—two parallel sofas in a living room suit you just fine. You can select the longest couches that will fit and that you can afford. People sitting on longer sofas can readily maintain desired distances from each other—not everyone wants to sit as close to other people as Adventurers do.

No matter what the design magazines are saying, make the coffee table between those two sofas as visually minimal as you can if you're an Adventurer—it's great if it's transparent, a color that blends with the color of the upholstery on the couches, or a light colored metal such as chrome with glass, etc.; no solid-looking mahogany or "significant" coffee tables here. Also, don't put more than a few objects on that coffee table; limit your accessorizing to one inspirational (and slight) book, for example.

Homes that support Adventurers are relatively high-energy places. Being revved up psychologically makes us all more conscious of how close we are to others and intent on establishing our own territory. As an Adventurer, you need to make sure your guests have the tools they need to create temporary territories. For example, a side table near a chair where a visitor can position their drink helps someone claim a space.

Furniture in an Adventurer's home should be moveable, because Adventurers need the flexibility to turn their living room into a yoga studio, dance floor, or the headquarters for their latest business venture. Adventurers will change the places where they live to suit their immediate needs whether it is easy to do so or not. If modifications can't be made gracefully, an Adventurer's home will look distressed.

Make sure that there are plenty of lamps in your living room if you're an Adventurer—gobs of rich golden light will make you and all your guests better conversationalists and more cheerful. Also, you'll like the fact that you can change the lightscape by varying which lamps are turned on together.

Adventurers socialize best when there are no barriers between them and the people with whom they're talking; many of the people who will be in their homes will either have a similar desire for "barrier-free" talks and/or know and accept their *modus operandi*. Every so often, however, a naïve newbie may find their way into an Adventurer's home, and the lack of furniture between them and the person they're talking to may be too much for them. The newbie will need a chair with arms. This should ideally be placed just beyond the ends of the two parallel sofas or in a similar sort of spot, so that the person sitting there will be at a comfortable distance from people sitting at the end of the sofas.

Adventurers need an out for anyone in their living room whose PlaceType makes them feel tense there. In the best sort of Adventurer living room, the stressed visitor can sit in an armchair positioned with a fireplace or similar interesting and large object in easy view, and the visitor can then "separate" psychologically by looking at that fireplace, fish tank, sculpture, or something else. They can let their eyes drift to that focal element, when they need a break from their colleagues. That living room focal point needs to be so inherently interesting that looking at it seems like a natural thing to do and not rude.

DINING ROOMS FOR ADVENTURERS

Since entertaining is important to Adventurers, and having people into their homes often involves food and meals, Adventurers need to make sure that their dining rooms support their PlaceType but don't overwhelm others.

As an Adventurer, you should combine several patterns that are moderately visually complex in your dining room. Patterns that are moderately visually complex feature a limited number of families of hues and shapes, three of each. Using more than three patterns together produces a relatively intense sensory experience—one pattern on seat cushions, another on drapes, and another somewhere in the dining room is enough. When you use several different patterns, each one should be in similar or complementary colors. This ensures your mix will add energy and minimize chaos.

When you're selecting wallpapers to go on your walls, remember that those with smaller scale patterns make rooms look larger than they will if you use larger scale ones; when lots of people are around, seeming larger is generally a great idea.

Ann relishes selecting dining room chairs without arms, but a few with arms will make people from some other PlaceTypes feel comfortable. Ann also needs to choose a round dining table, one that will accommodate the number of people she would generally seat at the table for a dinner party will fit into her dining room. If that doesn't work, she should go with an oval shape. Adventurers like to make eye contact during meals, and no shape gives you as much eye-to-eye access as a round table. Avoid rectangular tables if you're an Adventurer. The chairs at the short ends of the table, the mom and dad seats in every 60s sitcom, are associated with hierarchy; even having them available throws off the social dynamic that Adventurers enjoy. If you're an Adventurer, don't put chairs on the shortest sides of the table if you are using a rectangular table.

Adventurers enjoy surrounding themselves with design elements such as furnishings that are different from those normally seen among their circle of friends. So select interesting but comfortable chairs and unusual, but ergonomically appropriate, pieces of flatware. As an Adventurer, you relish investing in as many "uncommon" furnishings as you can afford.

KITCHENS FOR ADVENTURERS

Kitchens can be hard for Adventurers to design. They need to accomplish certain standard tasks there, and those activities lead to specific functional design requirements—but Adventurers like to do the unusual. They also dislike being separated from other people in their homes, and usually, particularly in older homes, kitchens are "a room apart."

If you're an Adventurer, you can include glass panels in any doors that need to be closed regularly—for example, to keep pets out of certain areas of the house. Kitchen doors often need to be closed, so glass panels in them can be highly desirable. The panels will lengthen sight lines and make it easier for you to feel involved with what's going on elsewhere in your home while you're in the kitchen.

Use shiny surfaces on woodwork and floors in kitchens and throughout your home if you're an Adventurer, but temper those shiny floors with rugs to prevent people both from "glaring out" and falling down. If you're an Adventurer, consider using high gloss paint on kitchen walls, if they're in great shape (since shiny paint highlights every imperfection on a surface). Mirrors and metals also add glossy surfaces that Adventurers welcome.

Pots hanging from the ceiling near the stove are also desirable, if the pots don't interfere in any way with entertaining guests or cooking. Shiny countertop canisters are another way to get tools out where they're handy, and if only a few are used, the level of visual complexity remains acceptable.

As an Adventurer, you want to be able to interact with your guests as you cook—if there's no way for this to happen, you need to feed your guests with delicacies prepared in advance or with take-out treats delivered to your home at just the right moments. You won't separate yourself from your guests, so don't plan menus or activities that require it.

There are several ways to keep guests close as you cook. Kitchen islands were probably invented by an Adventurer; they are a great command post for one. Seats in your kitchen, whether at a bar or not, work. A window cut into the wall between your kitchen and wherever people congregate in your home can also be a good way to stay in contact with other people. Adventurers enjoy being the entertainer-in-chief and using spaces efficiently.

OFFICES/STUDIES FOR ADVENTURERS

If you're an Adventurer, you love the idea of doing multiple things at once, but don't design for multitasking. No one can successfully do two tasks at the same time. As an Adventurer, if your job requires you to focus, as Ann's does, you need an office physically separated from socializing and relaxing spaces. Also, if your PlaceType is Adventurer, orient yourself toward views of nature or art depicting nature while you work. As an Adventurer, you push yourself to energy-draining extremes, so it is important that you be able to see something natural when you need to restock your mental energy. If all else fails, add a full, leafy plant about a foot tall to your desktop.

Adventurers, paint the walls of your offices a light sage green—greens have been linked to creative thought, which is important in many jobs, and a light sage green will put you as an Adventurer in the right mood to do knowledge work.

What kind of wood should Ann select for her office furniture? One with a clearly defined grain. Adventurers should scent their offices purposefully, keeping in mind the psychological implications of various smells noted earlier.

If you're an Adventurer, you need to be particularly concerned about storage in your office. You are very focused on achieving what you want to accomplish and are relatively easily stressed by clutter. Solid doors on bookshelves and other storage spaces keep the stuff in them out of view. As you battle clutter and disorder, don't remove all of the photos and other memory laden objects from your environment; keep a few around, say half a dozen. Customizing a space so that it tells your story to you and others boosts mood, which, as you'll recall from Chapter 2, is a very good thing.

Adventurers, make sure your office chair is comfortable for long-term sitting, and, if possible, add a standing desk to your office. You work hard if you're an Adventurer, but a painful back is a distraction that's almost impossible to ignore.

As an Adventurer, you enjoy textures from floors to walls, but don't forget a chair pad for your office chair. You don't want to be distracted from the task at hand by chair wheels that are stuck in carpeting.

RETREATS FOR ADVENTURERS—AT-HOME SPAS AND BEDROOMS

Places to relax are very important to an Adventurer's mental health. Bedrooms on a different floor from the main living areas can be a particularly good idea for Adventurers, because such bedrooms help them ease into a less social and more solo frame of mind.

Adventurers are high-energy souls, but even the most enthusiastic Adventurer needs to decompress during the day—even if only to fall asleep at night. A soothing shelter aligns with the previous experiences and current objectives of the people who are most likely to use it. If you're an Adventurer, make sure the design of your bedroom and bathroom supports experiences you associate with quiet relaxing, whether those are lying in a sunny spot and reflecting on the week, a gentle trouncing in a jetted bath, a long steam, or uninterrupted meditation in a still tub. Call these experiences to mind with colors, textures, scents, and so forth.

If you're an Adventurer, you cherish the unusual, but don't abandon old favorite pillows, area rugs, etc., when you redo spaces or remodel. Familiar things add comfort to a place, and even you need comfort every once in a while. Ann, for example, always makes sure she can see her grandmother's rocking chair from her bed. As an Adventurer, you're interested in the latest bed technology—the mattresses that can help you fall asleep faster and stay asleep longer, for example. So check them out.

The color palette for Adventurer bedrooms is slightly more energizing than might be found in the bedrooms for other PlaceTypes but is still generally calming. Accent colors in these bedrooms may actually be saturated and not very bright as long as the areas covered are small and number half a dozen or less. A scattering of rectangular shapes, in mirror or bed frames, for example, and multiple textures can also be used in Adventurers' bedrooms. Use wood with visible grain in furnishings and on other surfaces in your bedroom if you are an Adventurer, because it calms and has an appropriate level of visual complexity.

Adventurers need to be attentive to the scene they will view inside their bedroom while falling asleep; it should not be visually complex. If the budget and space allow, consider adding an electronic or alcohol fireplace or a fish tank to the master bedroom. Watching flames or fish is as effective a stress buster as a view outdoors.

Although Adventurers are often not keen on having curtains, sometimes the layout of your neighborhood or apartment building can make window treatments a requirement, not an option. A good way to please the neighborhood council and yourself, if you're an Adventurer, is installing colored Venetian (or similar) window blinds. The blinds can be lowered at crucial times but generally are pulled up out of sight, so they are effectively invisible for most of every waking day. Even Adventurers need to sleep sometimes, and, when they are dozing, blinds will also keep out neighborhood light.

Particular scents will help us relax, and if you're an Adventurer you should make sure that one of the restful fragrances listed in Chapter 2 is used in your retreat. Using design, you can create homes where daring Adventurers can be happy campers.

Guardians

MEET A GUARDIAN

Greg is a Guardian. Greg is everyone's favorite uncle—even after he settled down with kids of his own. Greg has a positive influence on the lives of those he encounters.

Guardians lead edited, organized lives. As a result, pieces of furniture, etc., can often move from one room to another in a Guardian's home, not because every room is filled with a collection of interesting things (like an Adventurers' home), but because each room highlights the Guardian's traditional styling consistency.

If you're a Guardian, you prefer to live in an apartment or home with rectangular rooms where Western furniture can be readily arranged. No positioning beds so their headboards block windows, if you're a Guardian. Guardians aren't interested in trying to squeeze an informal eating space into the wide hallway just outside the kitchen. An Adventurer would do so instantly as long as the spaces in their home remained useable and orderly.

Guardians have a yen for togetherness, like Adventurers. Unlike Adventurers, they don't crave spaces that have a novel or unusual twist; but Guardians do want their homes to keep up with changing household needs. Guardian homes should be full of lively sensory experiences. While Adventurers would add an intricately carved and painted wooden door from Bali to their dining room as a tabletop without hesitation, Guardians would purchase a highly polished table that packs the same sensory wallop as that Balinese table, but features smoother, easier to eat from, and more traditional surfaces. Guardians liberally use classic colors (e.g., navy blue and forest green), patterns, and other sensory elements.

As a Guardian, your best bet design wise is either an established décor, such as a tropical plantation look with rich dark woods, a modern style, or something else that has personal meaning for you. This means your home has a more unified look than that of an Adventurer, who is more focused on adding the unusual than coordinating the appearance of a number of rooms.

BEFORE YOU EVEN GET INSIDE

If you're a Guardian, you enjoy living in a lively neighborhood, just like Ann, but the ideal space to greet you outside your front door is not as bohemian as what Adventurers enjoy. You want to be able to venture out in the middle of a snowy Saturday afternoon and find wonderful chrysanthemums for that night's dinner party close to home, near the store where you can purchase everything you need to make that dinner a success.

Guardians benefit from having an expansive front porch, big enough for actually comfortable chairs and a few small scattered tables that can hold a couple of glasses of ice tea and a dish of lemon wedges. Front porches are a great place to entertain either planned or spontaneous guests. They also signal "friendliness" and build a connection to the local community, and that matters to Guardians. If you're a Guardian without a green thumb or any gardening skills, you should hire a professional landscape architect to create a climate appropriate and attractive front yard—that'll further encourage neighbor chats.

If your life makes living in the city more convenient and you're a Guardian, you should live in a building that's known to have a great sense of community, one with lobby areas that strengthen bonds between residents—perhaps because the door man is chatty or because there is a place where residents can connect regularly for events and topics of mutual interest.

LIVING ROOMS/FAMILY ROOMS FOR GUARDIANS

For Guardians, making a first impression that signals a classic sort of sociability is key. The spaces in Greg's home that matter most to him are those where people gather. He wants people in them to be comfortable, but that doesn't mean parked on a recliner watching a game. A space for lively conversations earns bonus points with Guardians.

Fireplaces are linked to socializing with others and are the sort of traditional element that appeals to Guardians. If you're a Guardian and find yourself fireplace-less, go to an architectural salvage house and purchase a mantel with the sort of strong rectangular forms and detailing that you find attractive. While you're waiting to have the mantel delivered and bolted to a wall in your living room, inlay brick, stone, or marble into the floor of the room in front of where the "fireplace" will be installed, using material consistent with the style of the room. Once the mantel is bolted in place, paint the wall behind the rectangular void in the middle of the new mantel black and add a fireplace screen in front of that rectangle. If the design of your home allows you to create a shallow faux firebox, do that and paint its interior black. Sure, people who look really closely at your new fireplace will be able to tell that it's not functional, but that won't really matter to you or your guests.

If you, like Greg, inherit Aunt Mary's difficult to perch on settee, you, like Greg, will consider passing it along to a cousin who'll cherish it forever, because all heirlooms are respected, even the ones you can't keep. Heirlooms that do work with your home—that fit into spaces, and so on—have pride of place in Guardian homes.

Greg's living room should be filled with a comfy assortment of loveseats, chairs, and couches. It you're a Guardian, select pieces of furniture that are relatively light in scale—that means you can rearrange them easily if no one else is around, if needed.

Guardians, like Adventurers, favor sofas, but not everyone who visits their home will, so a mix of seats is best. At least one comfortable single-person chair is needed in a Guardian living room so that people whose PlaceTypes are more at ease sitting in them have somewhere they feel comfortable to perch.

Greg feels best when all the seats in his living room are arranged in a rough circle. It works out well for Greg and others like him to have the focal point of the living room or family room in the middle of this group of chairs—a fireplace, a piece of art, etc., works well as a focal point. This gives people a graceful place to which to divert their eyes when they need to do so—focal points that are large enough to block eye contact get very low marks.

Guardians and Adventurers are high-energy types and often like to sit in rocking chairs. Rocking is a way to work off some pent-up energy without looking odd. Similarly, if you're a Guardian, you could add a glider on your front porch—gliders are really rocking sofas—as they combine movement with communal seating.

Upholstery and rugs feature well-known, relatively familiar patterns in spaces where Guardians feel comfortable. Those patterns will have more straight lines than curly ones, and they will blend because they share colors or forms (e.g., all feature abstract leaves). In an Adventurer's home, both upholstery and rugs may be "interesting" or "cool" but not coordinated in any other way; all design options selected are integrated in a Guardian's home. If you're a Guardian, add textures to a space with throws and pillows made from well-known materials or fabrics, such as wools and linens.

The same sorts of colors should be used in living rooms for Guardians as are found in those that support Adventurers. Since traditional design is well popular with Guardians, decorative elements, such as lamps, should have an established, solid feel. As a Guardian, you should have lots of tabletop and floor lamps in your living rooms because they allow lighting levels to be customized to exactly fit a situation. This makes guests and hosts more comfortable and makes it more or less likely that certain parts of the spaces will be used—we generally congregate in more brightly lit areas. Lampshades should be more square than rounded.

Art in Guardians' homes can feature people or nature scenes. The art that should line the walls of Guardian's room should be realistic and not abstract—more Kinkaid than Rothko. If you're a Guardian, you'd rather not have to explain your art to others—or yourself. Frames for photographs and pictures should be crisply tailored to complement the image being presented in the Guardians' homes. Rectangular frames and a dark rich wood are good choices when something more customized is too expensive or the image itself doesn't suggest a particular type of frame.

Guardians vigorously integrate family pets into their lives and don't worry about pet hair on their furniture—until company is about to arrive. So color coding pets and upholstery will help you, as a Guardian, keep tension levels low.

DINING ROOMS FOR GUARDIANS

Greg's dining room needs a traditional look that's missing from Ann's. Chairs and table and credenzas need to be coordinated. Guardians should purchase oval tables, not round ones like Adventurers. The ovals are more time-honored than rounds and still allow excellent eye contact.

At a dinner planned by Guardians, the table clothes, napkins, and plates should all have something in common, perhaps a similar color scheme or a theme (for example, botanical patterns), but they don't all need to match exactly. Similarly, the rugs and wallpapers in the room should support each other and a single theme—such as a nature enclave or an otherworldly geometric paradise.

Guardians need to think about purchasing furniture for their dining rooms that will remain comfortable throughout a multi-hour dinner party—they need to give their dining room chairs a "sit test," meaning that they should stay seated on the chairs in the furniture showroom for some time—fifteen minutes or so. Also, as a Guardian, you have to remember that not everyone is as active as you may like to be; consider the comfort of your larger size friends as you select dining room chairs.

Curtain rods can make a statement, and, if you're a Guardian, they should signal tradition. That means that for Guardians, there should be geometric forms as end caps on your curtain rods (e.g., pyramids and cubes), not birds or orbs.

If you're a Guardian like Greg, you can spring for chair rails with paneling below in your dining room. This combination adds the visual richness you crave to your dining room, particularly when the lower section of the walls is papered and the upper portions are painted in a complementary color. All moldings and baseboards should have angular and/or geometric designs.

Throughout their home, Guardians are likely to be happiest if they choose environmentally responsible materials. Their choices for wood floors should be environmentally responsible. Natural fibers are a good choice for Guardians; they'll likely remain popular for a long time to come and are readily available.

KITCHENS FOR GUARDIANS

Kitchens for Guardians are places to prepare foods that they love and need. Efficient and effective layouts, appliances, and other culinary accessories are required.

The kitchens of Guardians are organized; cabinets and drawers can be customized for their contents with special trays that cradle pieces of silverware or jars of spices.

All the cabinets in a Guardian's kitchen should be coordinated, not only with each other but also with the furnishings in the entire open living space that Guardians should endeavor to create or support in their home. Clear glass can be used in the front panels of a few of the cabinets to promote order and organization, but only a few panels can be transparent or stress-inducing clutter will be created.

Granite counter tops can be a good choice for Guardians; the patterns and shine please them, and the surface can be useful when pastries and similar projects are in the works. Utilitarian design is important to Guardians.

Kitchen islands are great for gathering and entertaining, and kitchens in which Guardians will be happiest will have one. If islands aren't possible for some reason, then a bar (breakfast or otherwise) around which people can cluster should be installed or a table included in the kitchen. Spaces where people can sit and eat while making eye contact are really important to Guardians, so eating may have to happen outside the main part of the kitchen, perhaps in the dining area, if kitchen space is tight. In the sort of home that'll please a Guardian, that dining area and the kitchen will be open to each other, anyway.

OFFICES/STUDIES FOR GUARDIANS

Guardians' offices need to be separated by walls and a door from the rest of the house if any work is going to get done in them. Guardians favor a traditional look and task-supportive design. Wooden furniture and desk chairs with a classic design are good options for Guardian offices. Guardian diplomas—all of them—can be neatly and conservatively framed and mounted where visitors can see them.

Neither Adventurers nor Guardians find curtains very important, and forgoing curtains in their offices may mean that Guardians have a better view of any nature that happens to be outside. Guardians should line up their desk with the window that looks out on the most nature. Going curtain-less also means that there's more daylight in a Guardian's office, and that means work performance is likely to be good.

Since Guardians prefer sofas to single seat chairs, they should add a sofa to their office if at all possible. If you're a Guardian, you can stretch out on the sofa and talk on the phone or sit beside visitors. It's important that whenever possible offices have an alternate chair or sofa for use on occasions when change-of-pace seating is necessary; that alternative can help keep people in their offices and at work. An important way to both reap some health benefits and work some variety into the offices of all PlaceTypes, Guardian and otherwise, is to add a standing height work surface.

If you're a Guardian, it's important that your office has enough storage to keep papers and tools not in current use out of view. If the space is cluttered with papers and supplies, a Guardian's performance will suffer.

RETREATS FOR GUARDIANS—AT-HOME SPAS AND BEDROOMS

Guardians need more time-honored sorts of retreats than Adventurers. Guardians must keep their homes clutter free, and they are happiest when possessions are tucked into bureaus, closets, armoires, or drawers—so these sorts of furniture must be available in their bedrooms as well as closets and bathrooms. All of those bureaus and armoires in use in a Guardian's bedroom should have the same finish and/or color.

Guardians prize order and getting rid of the crush of stuff that can haunt so many bedrooms, but that doesn't mean that there should be nothing on display in their rooms—don't be *too* ruthless at paring back the clutter if you're a Guardian. Don't put away your collection of perfumes or colognes that you use every day—keep it out on a dresser, shelf, or vanity top. The same might be true of a collection of scarves or ties— the bright silks provide the kind of pop that Guardians adore. Those scarves and ties should be displayed on a rack or hooks—no jumbly baskets here. If you're a Guardian, your bedroom should only feature one or two modest sized collections. They can't pack every flat surface.

If you're a Guardian like Greg, you enjoy being around shiny things. Surfaces, even in your retreats, should be polished to a glossy glow. Guardians and Adventurers should use the same colors in their bedrooms and bathrooms.

If you're a Guardian add thick, cuddle-your-toes carpets in your bedroom and bath. Luxurious towels and bed linens are worthwhile expenditures if you're a Guardian—as long as they're made out of materials found somewhere in nature, i.e., natural textile fibers like cotton.

A bathroom tub, jetted or otherwise, is something that Guardians can enjoy if their busy schedules allow them to take the time out for long soaks. Set up a relaxation station with soaps, sponges, and reading material to support your breaks in a steamy scented tub, if you're a Guardian and have some time for regular "decompression" baths. Guardians prize the pleasant scents of assorted soaps, etc. The entire soaking experience can help distract Guardians from the complexities of their lives outside the tub.

Guardians lead intense, dynamic lives, and the right sort of home design boosts their well-being.

CHAPTER 6

INVESTIGATORS AND SAGES—SPACES FOR INTELLECTUALS

Investigators and Sages live their best lives in homes and offices where the vibe is calm, understated, and contemplative. Their homes are their laboratories for happiness. While Enthusiasts live very much in the world, and relish the sensory experiences they have there, Intellectuals have a rich mental life, and the place that they live shouldn't distract them from it. Less is much more for Intellectuals. Too much going on outside their heads is bad for keeping track of what's going inside those noggins.

- The most important single feature for Investigators and Sages to look for when they're sizing up new homes are clearly separated spaces for as many members of the family as possible. Although some Investigators and Sages may be able to psychologically survive living in a home with an open-plan family room and kitchen, none will thrive in a home where they don't have clearly established territories and real privacy when they want it. That means spaces where they can sit and not see anyone else, and, in the best possible world, also not hear anyone else unless they want to because there's a door that can be open or closed as desired. And the hallways that connect those clearly delineated living and sleeping spaces need to be wide enough so that people walking in opposite directions don't intrude on each other's space by brushing against each other.

- Investigators and Sages clearly differentiate the public and private spaces in their homes, unlike Enthusiasts. Unless you are a *very* good friend, don't expect to be invited into a bedroom to watch a movie, even if the video screen there has the highest definition.

- Spaces where Investigators and Sages live their desired lives have built-in flexibility and will be changed as the activities they support evolve. Many Intellectuals are quick to work directly with the places that surround them—they rewire, rearrange, and reconfigure readily.

- Intellectuals are unconcerned with a room's official function—they'll use it as they see fit—which can make house hunting much easier for them as long as they don't succumb to social pressure and use a space only as its official label dictates. Intellectuals don't care if a space is officially a dining room or a walk-in closet—if a yoga studio or a meditation room is needed, that's how the area will be used.

- Intellectuals need to develop spaces that are efficient. In an efficient home, kitchens are laid out so that food can be prepared without bumping into guests or counter stools, for example.

- Intellectuals like their homes to actually support the task at hand, whether that's monitoring and managing the temperature in the house or helping prepare a major presentation. Furniture in Intellectual homes needs to be light enough in scale so it can be picked up or pushed into whatever places it can best serve its owner's current needs. Even better than having to push furniture from one place to another is furniture that, when needed, might serve two or more purposes well. A coffee table that can be adjusted to various heights above the floor can help a single space be multipurpose, and Intellectuals value furniture that provides that sort of useful variety, even if it may only be needed in the future. At standard coffee table height, an adjustable table can be a convenient perch for cocktails and bowls of peanuts. Raised a little higher, it can be a dining surface for people seated nearby or a space for crafting or playing cards.

- Intellectual homes need to be well equipped to store things—pens and papers, pots and pans, and everything else that finds its way into an Intellectual abode. Random storage is not the objective; trunks and chests into which things are thrown willy-nilly don't support Intellectuals. Storage needs to be more systematized with bins the same size as the collection of items to be stored, for example.

- Spaces where Intellectuals live their best lives are simple and unadorned, with no intricately carved moldings or picture frames, no ruffles, and no collection of porcelain pigs on the mantel. The dilemma for Intellectuals is that the sorts of environments that they enjoy can seem too stark and unusual for others to feel comfortable. The most straightforward ways to make guests feel welcome is for the Intellectuals to add music, warm lighting, soft nubby textures, plants, scents, and maybe an aquarium or a small tabletop fountain to a living room or dining room when guests are expected.

- Intellectuals should carefully investigate and then purchase objects and finishes that age well—no skimping on sofa cushions that quickly lose their fluff or drawers that don't slide smoothly. Finishes in Intellectuals' homes should be matte, not shiny, and mirrored surfaces should be avoided. Intellectuals enjoy living in spaces filled with natural materials. If you're an Intellectual, make sure that there are golden-hued hardwood floors throughout your home and on furniture whenever possible. Colors used should be deeply relaxing, and this often means colors that are very unsaturated and relatively bright. When colors are used in combination, they should be near each other on the color wheel—blues and greens, not reds and greens, for example.

- In Intellectuals' spaces, you should see more straight lines than curvy ones, just like in Enthusiasts' homes. And as in Enthusiasts' homes, the most desirable staircases are more rectangular than curvy, but in Intellectuals' homes they are simpler, with no unnecessary embellishments required.

- Curtains that hang straight down—with no flounces—are first choices for Intellectual homes, as are blinds that disappear or fold into compact accordions at the top of a window frame. Unlike Enthusiasts, Intellectuals will happily use curtains. It's important for them to remember how important sunlight and views outside are to mental health.

- Intellectuals do an excellent job preserving family traditions, both physical heirlooms and relationships between family and friends. They relish being the current custodians of something that's been in the family for decades, and they should go out of their way to display these items in prominent, conversation promoting locations.

- Intellectuals aren't generally couch potatoes. They like to be physically active, and homes situated near running and walking paths or with space to work out inside are good choices for Intellectuals.

- Since Intellectuals provide few clues for others to read, they need to be very focused when designing private spaces such as bathrooms—guests who find their way into them will be looking for insights there that they feel shed light on what the owner of that space values.

- Each of us has a dominant sense. If you're an Intellectual, it is particularly important that you identify it and make sure that home design is being managed accordingly. If you're an Intellectual and your dominant sense is olfactory, make sure relaxing smells are in place in areas where you'd like to relax, for example.

Investigators

MEET AN INVESTIGATOR

Isabelle is an Investigator. Like any good Investigator, Isabelle is always curious about new ways of thinking and living, and the design of her home must be flexible enough to incorporate whatever she finds desirable. Investigators may choose to live in very mechanized green homes, for example, if being green is important to them.

Investigators are freethinkers, and their homes should say that in both form and function. The sensory experience in these spaces should be understated, and the spaces can be inventively designed.

People looking at the sorts of environments where Investigators thrive might characterize them as having a "sparse sophistication." Investigators generally seem to have a great design sense, which isn't surprising considering they need to (and do) carefully consider each design-related decision and become educated about issues that interest them.

To make just the right single statement, Investigators may themselves craft the items displayed in their homes—massive store-bought flower arrangements are not welcome, for instance, but a few exquisite and carefully arranged blooms precisely positioned in the perfect vase are warmly received. To support this craftiness, Investigators may need a space in their home where they can craft out. The sort of space they'll need will depend on their interests. Metalworking and welding require a garage type space; paper folding can be done anywhere that's dry.

Investigators are keen on repurposing things they don't want to use in their earlier incarnations into ones that they can currently use. A workbench may, with a little tweaking, become a striking bathroom vanity. A former horse trough can become a planter.

Repurposing, however, always needs to be done in alignment with the rectilinear and spare design aesthetic that Investigators favor. No matter how exquisite it is, Investigators won't transform a curvy, intricately carved credenza into a bathroom vanity. In different contexts, Investigators may define quality in various ways; for example, something may have been made in an environmentally responsible way or may be a masterpiece aesthetically.

Investigators need to preserve empty spaces in their homes, although this sort of environment can make other Place-Personalities tense. Having just a few pieces of furniture in a living room is great for Investigators. If you are an Investigator, you find it relaxing to be in a place with lots of white space around objects. Don't be pressed to add more stuff to a space if you're an Investigator, just because people with some other Place-Personalities would or because TV shows and magazine articles make it look like you should. You are the best judge of when a space seems to have enough stuff in it. Trust your own instincts.

An Investigator's homes should be automated to the extent that the technology available promotes efficient home management—and that individual technical aptitude permits.

BEFORE YOU EVEN GET INSIDE

Investigators should live in places where their home is clearly separated from the homes of their neighbors. Investigator aren't social outcasts—far from it—but they just aren't that driven to meet the people who live near them. This makes Investigators good candidates for living in places such as old warehouse districts that are in the earliest stages of being converted to residential lofts, as well as desert retreats or other places where there just isn't much community spirit and few attempts to develop it via barbeques and holiday parties.

Investigators create places that are different from their neighbors, but they use a much more restrained aesthetic when doing so than Enthusiasts. Isabelle and Ann are both relatively conscientious and open to experience, and therefore there are similarities in their preferred environments, but Isabelle's internal world is rich and powerful while Ann's is not. Isabelle prefers that the physical environment in her home be restrained because this helps her maintain the level of environmental stimulation in which more introverted people thrive.

LIVING ROOMS/FAMILY ROOMS FOR INVESTIGATORS

Since Investigators like Isabelle prefer a streamlined aesthetic, the more light that can come from fixtures built into the structure of the home, the happier they'll be. If you're an Investigator, install zones of overhead lights and wall sconces, carefully planned so that anticipated activities such as reading, eating, or DIY pursuits are appropriately lit. High-tech tensor style lights are the sort that Investigators should select when task or ambient lighting is required in addition to the lights built into the walls and ceiling.

Investigators can minimize moldings and trim on the walls in their homes. Craftspeople may try to get you to add these elements if you're an Investigator, because they make it easier to do construction as the moldings cover floor to wall and ceiling to wall joints, which can be time-consuming to execute well—but resist.

The sorts of fireplaces enjoyed by Investigators are very different from the elaborate ones favored by Adventurers. Fireplaces for Investigators should be simple finished openings in walls. A slab of some natural material above the opening can serve as a mantel, if one is even added—it doesn't need to be.

If you're an Investigator, you should select furniture for your living room that has a pared down, rectilinear form. You should create a harmonious, uncomplicated look for your living room and the furnishings that you need to create the sort of unique, high style place where you will flourish are often available only from independent makers.

For Investigators, a coffee table can actually be an upholstered ottoman or wood in a nearly natural state with an uneven surface, since smooth level planes aren't required to display objects. Coffee tables chosen should have a real presence.

Select a few very unique objects to customize your space, and don't feel bound by conventions about what sorts of things you should display if you're an Investigator— it's OK to transform an empty bomb casing picked up from beside the road during a vacation in Laos into an umbrella stand or to use the polished stump of the tree that held up a childhood rope swing as an end table, though Investigators can run the risk of looking like strict museum directors to other PlaceTypes if their displays are too sparse.

If you are an Investigator, make sure that your living room, dining room, or kitchen can support your hobbies if you don't have another space in your home to transform into "Hobby Land." If you enjoy listening to or playing great music with others, make sure you have a place in your house where you can easily do so. Design your living room so that it has the furnishings, lighting, and other attributes (such as soundproofing) that are required. Similarly, if you collect or make art, make sure that there is a space in your home where you can display the carefully selected pieces that are important to you.

Homes for Investigators should contain green leafy plants. If your living room doesn't have much natural light, grow lights may be required.

DINING ROOMS FOR INVESTIGATORS

Investigator dining rooms need chairs that have arms and are grouped around a rectangular table. When Investigators prefer to dine in a group without a clear leader, all the dining room chairs can be arranged along the long edges of the table. Investigators prefer to place fewer chairs around a dining table than Enthusiasts, and they should increase the standard mid-chair back to mid-chair back distances of thirty-two to thirty-four inches by approximately another ten inches, if the size of their table allows.

If you are an Investigator like Isabelle, you should stock your dining room with unadorned linens and placemats. Clear glasses and simple light colored plates that make the food to be eaten the star of the show are good choices for Investigators.

Plates and utensils not currently in use need to be stored out of view. If you are an Investigator, you should buy a credenza or buffet with solid fronted doors that keep visual complexity in check by hiding objects from view. And, if you are an Investigator, you may have quite a few objects that need to be shielded from your view—you may have collected plates, cups, and silverware designed specifically for the sorts of foods you enjoy, such as sushi. After a while, it all really does add up, and a jumbo cabinet, say one with simple lines that look Scandinavian, is required.

Dining room rugs keep sound levels low and echoes in check, so make sure that you invest in monochrome or nearly monochrome rugs in colors darker than the wall of the dining room. A lower and flatter nap on that rug will make it easier to keep the floor clean. Eating under a sparely designed chandelier with unusual rectangular elements such as carved crystal drops is Investigator heaven.

KITCHENS FOR INVESTIGATORS

The kitchens of Investigators should be efficient cooking zones, filled with the specialized tools that make cooking a breeze—and each tool must have a clear home in a cabinet or drawer to which it is returned after use. Appliance garages can be a good way to keep everything neat yet accessible in these kitchens. An appliance garage is a cabinet at the back of a counter whose front panel slides up and down like a garage door. Investigators are awestruck when they see Julia Child's kitchen, now in the Smithsonian, because she and her husband developed a pot and pan organization system second to none. They drew a line around the exterior of each pot and pan when all were hung in the configuration that took up the least space on the wall of their kitchen. The outlines enabled them to quickly return a pot or pan to the best possible location on the wall after use.

Investigators may invest in professional style kitchens because they like to prepare recipes that require the sorts of tools and space usually used by people who cook for a living. Catalysts' homes may have professional, high-quantity production kitchens as well, but they have installed such kitchens so they can prepare meals for many people at the same time.

Cabinets should have solid doors in Investigator kitchens. Investigators don't like or need to see what's inside—they know what's there because their kitchen was planned and is maintained according to that plan. Self-closing doors and drawers get positive reviews from Investigators.

Investigators have no need for islands unless they are functional—for example, that may be where the amount of available counter space dictates that the cooktop lives. If you're an Investigator, you may find that you can really streamline the cooking process by placing a sink or work surface, for example, in the middle of the kitchen.

If you're an Investigator like Isabelle, use mainly matte finishes in your kitchen and try to eliminate shiny metal ones whenever possible. Concrete countertops can be good choices if they are in shades of gray that might actually be found in the concrete of building foundations and they're not buffed until shiny. Investigators enjoy using new and different materials. The color scheme of Investigator kitchens should feature warm, unsaturated, and relatively bright colors.

The kitchens of Investigators can become too "mechanistic" to be hospitable. To counter this, include a few curved edges (on the backs of kitchen chairs, for example) throughout the space. Find space for a comfortable in-kitchen armchair for guests, if possible. Also, don't forget your own kitchen comfort if you're an Investigator—add rubber mats to stand on while you work to keep your back happy.

OFFICES/STUDIES FOR INVESTIGATORS

Offices for Investigators should contain just the tools they need to work well. Investigators often have extensive collections of books, or at least they did before the age of Nook and Kindle. Reviewing the books arrayed on bookshelves helps Investigators remind themselves of concepts that are important to them. These reviews, which are generally subconscious, flow best when the titles of the books are not obscured by cabinet doors. Besides the books on display, visual distractions must be kept to a minimum in Investigators' offices. Organization is easiest with cabinets and storage systems that do not have transparent panels.

Investigators should invest in effective cord management systems. Electrical cords winding their sloppy way across surfaces or tangled with others irritate them.

Golden light is a good choice here, particularly if an Investigator does a lot of business over the phone. Investigators' offices need landscape art on the walls that is somewhat abstract and several plants on waterproof surfaces.

RETREATS FOR INVESTIGATORS—AT-HOME SPAS AND BEDROOMS

Bathrooms for Investigators aren't crammed with stuff. Shampoos and lotions are carefully selected, for example, so there aren't oodles of also-rans that need a place to quietly decay until throwing them away seems justified.

If you're an Investigator, invest in a medicine cabinet that combines innovative features with enough storage space. For example, the best cabinet for you may have a mirror that doubles as a screen where you can project favorite nature photos.

Bathrooms for Investigators should have mainly rectilinear faucets, spigots, basins, and tubs. The shower stalls, basins, and tubs into which water will flow might use original materials; imagine a clear glass tub or features, and maybe that tub will scent the air, but not the bather, during baths. All items selected need to be carefully vetted as reliable and straightforward to maintain.

Investigators are likely to be interested in innovative self-care products, such as add-on bidet-type toilet seats that replace conventional toilet seats and similar products. Walls in Investigator bathrooms should be painted extremely relaxing colors (very unsaturated and light colors) and be smooth, not tiled or textured. People like Isabelle need to remember that they're more comfortable in spaces that they've personalized, and bathrooms are no exception. One or two personally meaningful objects, like an empty bottle of their dad's favorite cologne or a hairbrush with a family pedigree, can be on view in the bathroom even though, from a functional perspective, they're not necessary.

Investigators enjoy carefully organizing their closets, and a little time online or at home organization stores will turn up lots of useful organizational tools. Investigators are most comfortable in bedrooms where everything being stored can be tucked out of sight. If closet organizing systems can't handle the load, perhaps the closets available just aren't physically large enough to hold everything that needs to be organized, Investigators are very open to using nontraditional storage spaces, such as behind lounging chairs where no one can see stored items (really). If a platform bed with drawers can fit into an Investigator's bedroom, it's a good choice because the storage space underneath can come in handy, as will any space in window seats. Storage ottomans are an option for Investigator bedrooms as well since the ottomans can be used bedside.

Bureaus for clothes storage should be rectangular and modern in appearance. Investigators enjoy the clean look of drawers without hardware, including drawers that open when someone pushes on them gently. Picture frames and similar decorative elements should be relatively rectangular as opposed to curvy.

Investigators are happiest when they can use science and design to their advantage. They are particularly interested in new developments in these fields that can make their lives better in a way that's meaningful to them. Mattresses are now a hotbed of development, after having been relatively uninteresting, at least in terms of research, for some time. Investigators relish the idea of sleeping on mattresses that utilize the latest research findings and technology; for example, allowing each person sleeping in a bed to "tune" the mattress to the temperature they prefer for sleep.

Towels, sheets, blankets, you name it; linens and bedding selected should be designed for success in whatever role they play (for example, absorbing water) as well as a pleasure to use, with softness being one desirably pleasing trait to consider.

In an Investigator bedroom, bedside lights should be mounted directly to the wall at the optimal level for reading, which will vary with the height of the bed selected but generally be at eye level when the reader is reclined. This creates the sleeker look that Investigators cherish. Users should be able to adjust light levels so they are high enough for reading or low enough to create an intimate setting. Similarly, the state-of-the-art television sets that Investigators take pride in owning should be wall-mounted to reduce surface clutter and available for immediate spontaneous use.

To soften the ambiance in their bedrooms, Investigators should add a comfy overstuffed chair, probably club-like in style, to mesh with their generally rectangular look. "Club-like" is used here only to provide a very basic direction; desirable chairs will have cushions on their backs, sides, and seats that are shaped basically like laptops but are thicker because of all of the cushiony stuffing that make them so comfortable to sit on. Investigators enjoy furniture that's unusual, so a classic club chair might be too boring for use, even in a bedroom. The chair should be anchored by an adjoining small table for books and gadgets. Both the chair and the table should sit on an island of carpet that's different from the carpeting in the rest of the room and feels pleasantly sensuous under bare feet. Investigator bedrooms should feature colors that are light and not very saturated.

HALLWAYS FOR INVESTIGATORS

Isabelle and her kind should always be on the lookout for artwork that pleases them in galleries, at flea markets, or wherever they may find themselves. The mix of all they'll select can be eclectic (although landscapes and nature scenes are popular) and may be a little jarring if hung in a single room together. Hallways are perfect places for Investigators to display their art, however, as a single piece, or perhaps only a few, are visible at any one time. Investigators buy art that they like and has potential for long-term appreciation. They anticipate that their children may ultimately sell pieces of their art, but that they will keep it until death does them part. When art is displayed in a hallway, hallway lights should be similar to those found in any other gallery, lighting the art without damaging it.

Investigators are most comfortable in hallways where two people can walk past each other without touching, which means spaces used for displaying art and to connect areas in the home need to be relatively wide. Investigators live rich and rewarding mental lives; their best physical environments support their intangible needs well.

Sages

MEET A SAGE

In a space where Sages live their best lives, you'll never be overwhelmed by the décor or the number of other people present. Sages' spaces should use time-honored interior design but be supple enough so that users flourish today and tomorrow. A Sage's sofa shouldn't be unusual, and it won't be buried under a barrage of pillows of varying colors and textures, either. The sorts of places where Sam the Sage are comfortable are uncomplicated and calm. The homes where Sages thrive feel fresh, clean, and ordered. In a space where Sages feel comfortable, there may be few pieces of furniture, with each one present carefully considered before purchase.

Like everyone else, Sages need daylight to feel and perform at their best, but it's best if they can get their daily dose without seeing their neighbors and what they're up to. Skylights can be good choices for Sage homes because they can flood a home with daylight but not with views of other people. Sages, like all other humans, also need refreshing views. Sage homes should have extensive views of any natural spaces that are nearby; if there just aren't any, a fountain with gently moving water should be added in a place visible through the window, if possible, or inside on a tabletop. Realistic paintings and photos of landscapes should definitely be used in view-challenged homes.

Sages are concerned with the apparent cleanliness and upkeep of their homes. Laundry rooms need to be sleek and workbenches readily accessible for cleaning and repair tasks. Tools must be appropriately stored so they can function well and immediately. An organized closet containing mops and polishes is popular with Sages. They also should choose carpeting, flooring, upholstery, and other materials that wear well, are stain resistant, and are easy to keep looking good.

If you're a Sage, don't be pressured into buying the home your real estate agent thinks you should have, buy the one whose bones send you the messages you want to hear. Sages shouldn't purchase an open-plan home just because it may be easier to sell later. Although long sight lines through a home are important, Intellectuals feel more comfortable in a home where all shared areas are not in a single large room. If you're a Sage, search for a home whose architecture features straight lines and relatively restrained ornamentation. "Stately" is a good adjective to describe the architecture preferred by Sages.

BEFORE YOU EVEN GET INSIDE

Sam and his fellow Sages are not too interested in interacting with their neighbors and, if they must live near others, will try to do things such as relax outside without seeing them. Rural living can work out well for Sages, but they don't want to be an inconveniently long drive from where they work or other frequent destinations.

Sages are happier in homes with back patios or decks than in houses with front porches. If for some reason a home with a front porch is purchased, perhaps because of a particularly convenient location or a price that was too good to pass up, the decorating budget should be allocated to favor back patio or deck improvements. That means perfunctory spending on the front porch, perhaps to acquire the requisite chair indicating that the people within aren't psychopaths, with the bulk of the outdoor budget being spent on enhancing or building the back patio or deck.

ENTRYWAYS FOR SAGES

Entryways in Sage homes should feature classic elements such as a few crisply framed family portraits—not exuberant personal displays of travel souvenirs, children's art, or casual photos. Entryways are comfortable for visitors when they hold clues about the interests and values of people living in a home, but Sages have a tendency to pare down the possessions displayed so rigorously that visitors are confused. If you're a Sage, make your guests lives easier by sharing something with them that has meaning to you—even a single photo from your childhood can help!

LIVING ROOMS/FAMILY ROOMS FOR SAGES

Sages are happiest when sofas are few and far between and individual chairs are the most plentiful seating option in their living room. The chairs should be arranged so they are interspersed with substantial end tables and coffee tables. The tables should have a definite presence, as wooden furniture does, but be easy to reposition and repurpose. There should be no transparent glass coffee tables here.

Since Sages prefer to have single-person chairs in their living rooms, guests can't scrunch together to provide a couple of seats for latecomers or unexpected guests. For the infrequent occasions when there are more guests than chairs, Sages should keep a stock of comfortable cushions on hand and distribute them to later arriving people so they can find comfortable spaces on the floor to relax during conversations. Cushions also give guests a great deal of flexibility; people on them can sit close to or far from other guests, as they prefer.

The main colors in a Sage living room or family room should be not very saturated but fairly bright, such as light blue-grays and pale sandy browns. Colors used should be near each other on the color wheel (e.g., use blues and greens together). Rooms that feature several shades of the same color (for example, green) work well for Sages. Upholstery on furniture should be a single color, with perhaps flecks of another color or a simple pattern that makes any future stains harder to spot. Rugs and wallpapers should follow the same guidelines set for the upholstery. Rugs should be dark enough to anchor the space; they should be the darkest surface in the room.

The fireplace in a Sage's living room should feature natural materials such as slate and other stones, and mantels are optional here. Sages enjoy being in spaces where natural materials are plentiful, so stone should be used frequently in Sage homes, along with wood with a visible grain, cottons, and linens, for example. Hardwoods with a clear golden finish can be used on floors.

Sages can and should add art to their spaces. Sam can't resist a good landscape, and they should be plentiful on the walls of his living room and family room. The art on display may well be familiar to people who've taken Art History 101; Sages aren't interested in breaking new ground as far as art goes, they're interested in displaying the sorts of pieces that have stood the test of time.

Living room built-ins with solid, not transparent, doors should be used by Sages to corral their books and CDs. Built-in cabinets and bookshelves also often look more streamlined than freestanding shelves.

Sages can feel comfortable if their living room ceilings are a foot or two higher than the ten-foot limit mentioned in Chapter 2.

DINING ROOMS FOR SAGES

Sages should select dining room furniture that is relatively light in scale with many straight lines. Rectangular tables are best in Sages' homes, and dining chairs should have arms. A separate room for dining is desired, and if one is not available, the dining "room" should be clearly delineated using wall paint colors, flooring changes, etc. Furniture legs anywhere in Sage homes must be straight and functional: a lack of embellishments or enhancements such as curves or carvings is best. The furniture should be made of wood, not glass or metal, and the wood should have a light-colored finish with a visible grain.

A sideboard or credenza can be important to Sages because it keeps dishes of food from making the tabletop too cluttered; also, if dishes are placed on the sideboard after circulating among diners, individuals can retrieve additional helpings without bothering other people. Sages do best with dish storage behind solid wooden doors so things inside can't be seen and won't max out the visual complexity of the room.

Linens and plates for Sage dining rooms should have a simple and straightforward design; think unadorned Scandinavian pieces that are both minimalistic and rectilinear, the kind that might look at home in IKEA, with nary a decoration in sight. Simple is better and flashy is out.

Dining rooms are the one place in non-mansions where hanging light fixtures are expected, and Sages feel best if they choose light fixtures that will softly light a space and that have a relatively angular look. Like Investigators, Sages prefer that sound absorbing materials be used throughout their homes, so dining rooms may be carpeted and chairs upholstered.

KITCHENS FOR SAGES

Sages need to take the time to carefully consider all of the sorts of cooking that they'll do in their kitchen to make optimal use of the floor and counter space at their disposal. Sages should assess each appliance as if it's an engineering puzzle to be solved. Those that can make the best case for their effectiveness and efficiency in the context of the kinds of cooking they plan to do and the life they plan to lead should carry the day. For example, Sages who don't use many ice cubes should forgo refrigerators with in-door ice makers, while those who use lots of ice should purchase a refrigerator where ice cubes seem to fly into the in-door cube center. The appliances that make Sages happiest are those that are ergonomic and prevent unnecessary physical stress and strain on the cook. The finish on appliances should be matte.

Sages feel best in their kitchens if they're organized and there are very few objects on their countertops. If you're a Sage like Sam, you should make sure that there is adequate drawer and cabinet space in your kitchen to neatly accommodate all of your glasses, dishes, cutlery, and cooking equipment. Sages do not favor deviating from efficient "kitchen triangle" arrangements—kitchen-based socializing is much less important than efficient food production.

Sages can appreciate a central charging station for all of the portable electronics in their homes, and generally the most logical place to position it is in the kitchen. Having a central depot makes it easier to keep unsightly cords from corrupting the look of the entire home and means that portable devices have a single home so they're straightforward to find.

OFFICES/STUDIES FOR SAGES

Sage offices and studies should be well planned with lots of storage. Filing cabinets are probably necessary. Organizing is a very serious business for Sages.

Sages relish a cockpit style desk setup so that a swivel of a desk chair orients them toward different stretches of desktops, credenzas, and other tabletops. Sage desks should have drawers or compartments so that the tools Sages need in order to work well are close at hand but out of view. Items to be stashed include pens, scissors, and printer paper, just for starters. Office drawers and/or compartments also need to hide a paper management system. Somewhere close at hand, Sages may also need a paper shredder that is easy to use and empty. Sloppy electrical cords make Sages tense—they should invest in systems that keep cords well managed and out of sight.

All of the professional tools that Sages have at their disposal need to work well or be straightforward to fix. Sages like to live in an orderly world. Sages enjoy useful gadgets— particularly when they work.

RETREATS FOR SAGES—AT-HOME SPAS AND BEDROOMS

In successful Sage homes, bedrooms are sparingly furnished and contain only a few photographs, pieces of art, and other personally meaningful objects. The items present, however, should be important to the owner of the space, and the way they are displayed should indicate that respect. Each one should be placed where it is set apart from other objects. A single item, for instance, a photo or a pot made by children in arts and crafts class, should be placed so it can be seen and enjoyed from a variety of angles.

Organizers should purchase bedroom furnishings with straight lines and a traditional feel. A bed with squared-off posts at each of its corners can add a splash of style to the room without disrupting the overall aesthetic, for example.

Furnishings, linens, and draperies in a Sage's bedroom should be consistent with a well-established but relatively minimalist look, such as Shaker and the more modern design styles that built on the Shaker tradition. Whenever possible, any object in a Sage's bedroom should be made out of natural materials, whether it is a duvet cover or a drape. All fabrics should be unpatterned or have a simple geometric look. Curtains are high on a Sage's priority list, but Sages have no need for dust ruffles or tasseled curtain tiebacks. Walls should be painted or papered win a solid color, not patterns.

Sages with families can establish a "family-only" entertainment area in their master bedroom suite, complete with single-person chairs or cushions that can be used by family members as they gather in front of a flat-screen TV.

Bedrooms for Sages should have several leafy green plants with rounded leaves. Their pots should blend with the overall decorative scheme.

When Sages create spaces for guests, they need to plush them up to ensure that visitors feel welcome. That means, for example, that these spaces should include luxurious and sensuous blankets and carpets. To compensate for the austerity in the rest of the home, Sage guest rooms could include several pieces of curving furniture, perhaps a desk and chair whose legs gently bow, a round mirror with a carved and gilded frame, or a swooping lamp.

Bathrooms for Sages should have simple countertops and only minimal shiny surfaces and mirrors. Stone finishes are popular on floors and shower walls. So are natural materials in general, and their palette should be relatively light. Teak benches in showers should be used instead of plastic or metal ones. Sages' bathrooms need enough built-in storage to hold all of the health and beauty aids and keep items out of view. Sages enjoy traditional white bathrooms that are tiled—it's clear when they're clean, and they have a classic feel. Taps and tubs should not be curvy, and shower curtains or bath enclosures should be rectilinear and crisp. Sages should install showers and tubs with lots of functionality. If possible, that means multiple massaging showerheads and tubs that keep soaking water warm for a long time, for instance.

Sages live well when the design of their homes is carefully considered, restrained, and true to strong design traditions.

CHAPTER 7

MAVERICKS AND DYNAMOS—SPACES FOR CATALYSTS

Mavericks and Dynamos do well in homes that are lush and nurture links with other people.

- When they're looking for homes, Catalysts need to search for houses with large rooms that are open to each other and spaces where a number of people can be seated—homes that support entertaining. Supporting entertaining may require a kitchen with both a more public zone and an area that's a little more private where dirty pots and pans can escape view. French doors with lots of windows make it easy to see who's on outside patios and who's inside. They also make it easier for people to circulate at parties and prevent collisions that result in spilled drinks and ruined clothes. Houses with more windows work well for Catalysts, because all of those windows keep interior spaces from feeling crowded.

- Mavericks and Dynamos prefer spaces that are lush, with robust sensory experiences. Dynamos use conservative and traditional touches such as oriental rugs and other ornate but expected patterns throughout their homes, while Mavericks get their sensory fixes via Moroccan textiles, for example, and other less traditional design options. Mavericks are a daring PlaceType, and they enthusiastically incorporate unusual objects and design ideas into their homes and offices.

- Individual spaces are dedicated to particular uses and are not likely to be changed without careful deliberation. Heavier furniture and built-ins are accepted here.

- Catalysts may have a sentimental attachment to lots of objects—which can drive visual complexity to rise above comfort levels. Spaces where Catalysts will spend time should have horizontal surfaces on which they can place the photos and objects that are most personally meaningful, all in some kind of order—in cubby holes, for example. If you are a Catalyst, understand that rotating parts of your collection into and out of view will be best for your mental health.

- Mavericks and Dynamos are most relaxed and happy when they're in spaces with more curved elements than straight ones but which are a little more energizing than those favored by the population as a whole. This means they can invest in modern Chippendale-like sofas upholstered in bright, luxurious silks and swoopy, high-backed overstuffed chairs that are comfortable enough so that people want to hang out in them for hours. Catalysts can happily install drapes that actually do drape in gentle curves when pulled to the side of a window. They can select curtains that puddle or are a little longer than necessary so the extra material falls into graceful clumps on the floor. Catalysts may respond positively to window scarves, those long, long, generally gauzy strips of fabric that loop across the top of windows and cascade down their sides.

- Buying pieces (of furniture, or art, or something else) that might be passed to the next generation can be a waste of resources. Good enough for now is a philosophy that Catalysts endorse. Their focus isn't on things as much as on people and the good things others can bring into their lives.

- Structure, focus, and organization are not guiding forces in the lives of Catalysts, not because they can't structure, focus, and organize, but because they choose not to do so. Catalysts' home offices should be separated from the parts of their homes where other people may be hanging out by floor-to-ceiling walls and a door. Catalysts enjoy being with other people, and they mingle whenever they can. Socializing can win out over work if a Maverick or Dynamo can hear others' conversations. Make sure your office chair is comfortable for long-term sitting if you are a Maverick or a Dynamo. It can be too tempting for a Maverick or a Dynamo to wander around to get rid of a crick in his or her back or some other physical complaint—and not finish work that needs to get done. If you're a Catalyst, make sure you have a comfortable upholstered chair in your home office where you can sit for a change of pace from your desk chair. When Mavericks or Dynamos leave their offices to read comfortably or some other activity, the odds are good that they'll get diverted into a non-work activity. Mavericks and Dynamos can keep themselves on task by placing a lamp that creates a warm circle of light on their desktop that's large enough to illuminate what they're working on. That lighted circle will help them stay focused and keep from wandering—both mentally and physically.

- Catalysts have busy homes, and generally they're not interested in spending lots of time cleaning them. Catalysts may love carpet, but should choose floor coverings that have a low nap so that dirt doesn't get embedded in them. HVAC systems with great filters and vacuums that filter air are both good investments for Catalysts, as are generally darker flooring and countertops that won't show too much dirt and that will wear well.

- Catalysts can select houses where neighbors can possibly see into their homes.

- Catalysts are dedicated to leisure. This doesn't mean they don't put all that they have into doing their jobs well. It means that when they're off the clock, Catalysts enjoy having a good time. Not only are expansive patios and porches good places for Catalysts to more formally entertain, they're also great places to spend hours relaxing with a book, or, as is more probable for a Catalyst, with a set of good friends who've dropped by. Catalysts should make sure their homes have pleasant places to relax and watch movies and television, whether they have space in their home for a separate home theater or not. Catalysts will feel that every penny spent on these gathering spaces is well spent.

- Catalysts need to make sure that their home is in a location that supports their lifestyle; it needs to be close to their family and friends, and their circle of friends will quickly expand to include neighbors, new and old, known for a few months or a lifetime. If Catalysts can't be near family and friends for some reason, they should find a place to live near where they'll spend a lot of time, such as in the heart of the nearest city or near a place with a lot of pedestrian traffic, so they'll be able to get out and be around other people often. Catalysts like to spend time hanging out with family and friends, and, for some, socializing is their primary leisure time activity.

- If you're a Catalyst, you're probably not really interested in do-it-yourself projects. You'd rather spend your time doing other things. Don't buy a home where they'll be required. One positive repercussion of eschewing DIY projects is that you don't need to store the materials and tools required to complete them.

Mavericks

MEET A MAVERICK

The challenge for Mavericks is keeping their house from being overrun by people or things. Melissa and other Mavericks can create intense spaces filled with personal, emotional, sentimental elements that can appear somewhat sappy to people with other PlaceTypes.

Spaces that are rich in sensory experiences, that make it easy to interact with others as they nurture the soul, should be created by Mavericks. Mavericks should select furniture for their homes that has an innovative but sturdy feel, as chairs, tables, and sofas in their homes get a lot of use.

Since Mavericks can be unconventional in their design choices, the atmosphere in their homes can in some cases overwhelm visitors and seem wild and unpleasant. Mavericks need to carefully consider the ramifications of moving forward with all of their design ideas.

Since Mavericks are not big on spending time organizing their homes, storage facilities have to be really easy to use and hard to avoid. Mavericks need to get stuff out of view, so the storage options in their home should help with that—but Mavericks aren't overly concerned with the orderliness of their storage or their homes generally. So for example, to keep a Maverick's holiday wreath protected, it should be able to fit into a number of storage containers, not just the one tailored to its exact shape that Intellectuals would buy and love using. Mavericks aren't terribly concerned about being able to find things quickly or if items get jumbled. That means they could invest in large trunks and toy chest-like storage.

BEFORE YOU EVEN GET INSIDE

Mavericks like their front yards to draw people to their front door. They should have their front yards professionally landscaped, unless they have done a lot of gardening and can force themselves to pay attention to their landscaping and keep it looking good. Adding a bench to their front yard, together with anything else that will encourage people to linger in front of their home, sounds like a great idea to a Maverick.

Mavericks enjoy creating a front door experience that puts visitors in an upbeat mood. They may select doorbells that when pushed play songs that boost their mood and probably will be enjoyed by their guests. The doorbell should be paired with a door knocker—Mavericks don't want to miss any visitors if the power goes out.

LIVING ROOMS/FAMILY ROOMS FOR MAVERICKS

Mavericks are interested in thinking beyond the expected and are keen on socializing. A few decades ago, Mavericks were into beanbag chairs and conversation pits before anyone else. Now Mavericks can have spaces for Skype or FaceTime conversations with friends and grandkids built into their homes.

For now, living rooms and family rooms are the site of a lot of the socializing Mavericks do—both in person and virtually.

Living rooms for Mavericks should be organic and curvy, with furniture substantial in scale—but not so big that it can't be repositioned for big family gatherings with some planning. Decorative elements in a Maverick's living room such as moldings should be elaborate, curved, and unusual. That goes for frames, lamps, lampshades, coasters, and everything else.

Colors in Maverick living rooms can be relatively saturated and not very bright. Darker colors on walls make spaces seem smaller; to prevent claustrophobia, keep the colors used in Mavericks' living rooms a little lighter than those the Mavericks might initially select. Mavericks should choose upholstery, drape fabrics, and rugs with patterns, and multiple patterns can be used in a living room, as long as the space is roughly moderately complex visually. All patterns should have similar colors, however, to keep the space coherent. For example, each piece of furniture may be upholstered in a different fabric, but all may feature Kelly green, canary yellow, a warm cream, and bubblegum pink. (Using these colors together would actually be pretty dazzling, but just thinking about this sort of combination makes a Maverick's blood flow quickly.) Wallpapers can also be patterned.

Mavericks should have fireplaces enhanced by decorative elements such as curved rosettes. A mantel in a Maverick's living room needs to be wide and smooth enough to hold precious objects. The fireplace surround and mantel are a way for Mavericks to add more zest to their living room—shiny, eye-catching paint and materials can be used here in Maverick living rooms.

If the size and shape of the living room allows, Mavericks can place two sectional sofas facing each other. The goal is to have multiple pieces, with some at angles to others, that are arranged to make eye contact easy. If space is really tight in the living room, Mavericks should pair a single living room sofa with two or three (or more) chairs, with the number of chairs depending on the size of the space. Seats that find their way into a Maverick's home should be unusual whenever possible—either because of the way people sit on them, the upholstery fabric, the shape of the arms, the backrest, or something else.

Furnishings in Maverick homes may make use of unusual manmade materials. How about inflatable sofas? Mavericks would say, "Why not?" Many others would say, "No way."

Mavericks want visitors to be extremely comfortable everywhere in their homes, so they should purchase well-padded comfortable seats. Comfortable people are people who are happy to linger. Mavericks are interested in having a variety of available places to sit, as well. They should have a chair for their cousin with the bad back so he doesn't have to go home early, as well as furniture sized for extra small and extra large adult visitors.

While tchotchkes in the living rooms of Intellectuals are often chosen carefully to make particular statements, items on display in spaces favored by Mavericks are much more likely to have a personal, sentimental meaning. They need to be pruned regularly and thoughtfully arranged to prevent stress-inducing clutter. Mavericks who have real difficulty parting with stuff need closet-organizing systems that allow them to stash oodles of things out of sight: armoires in every room to hide their treasures and furniture with hidden storage capabilities, such as tables whose tops open on hinges to reveal storage space.

Some of a Maverick's family pieces can be used in unexpected ways—the antlers inherited from Cousin Bob may be used to hang visitor coats, or an elaborate umbrella stand from Aunt Mary may become the base for a side table featuring a top made out of a hostess tray.

Other PlaceTypes keep live plants in their homes, but that's not a good idea for Mavericks—one of the DIY projects they're not into is watering a plant often enough to keep it alive. Mavericks can be happy with artificial plants in their living room. Plastic plants that look plastic are still a no-no, even for Mavericks; the fake foliage in a Maverick's living room should pass for real.

The art in a Maverick's living room should start conversations. Nothing gets people talking as quickly as unconventional art, so Melissa and other Mavericks love it. A painting of a purple cow can hang over the couch, and a color block painting may be positioned over the fireplace. A classic landscape with a twist—say metallic trees—can find its home between the two windows. Mavericks have a lot of art and design sense and are more open to new types of art than most.

Mavericks' homes should include an outside gathering place, a sort of fair-weather living room, where Mavericks can host meals and other events. These spaces may contain fire pits—Mavericks love the way a good fire draws people in close.

DINING ROOMS FOR MAVERICKS

Mavericks need lots of space at their dining room table, and, in Western homes, the room and table shape combination that allows the maximum number of chairs is long and rectangular. To seat all of their guests, Mavericks prefer to use either chairs without arms or benches that stretch along the long sides of the tables. Dining room chairs should have cushions.

Maverick dining rooms should create a luxuriously sensual experience for diners. There may be an extravagant, sparkly chandelier hanging in the center of the room and an intricate embroidered tapestry, for instance. The linens, rugs, drapes, and wallpapers should feature saturated and warm, but not very bright colors.

Lines, whether they're in rugs and wallpapers or table legs, should mainly be curved.

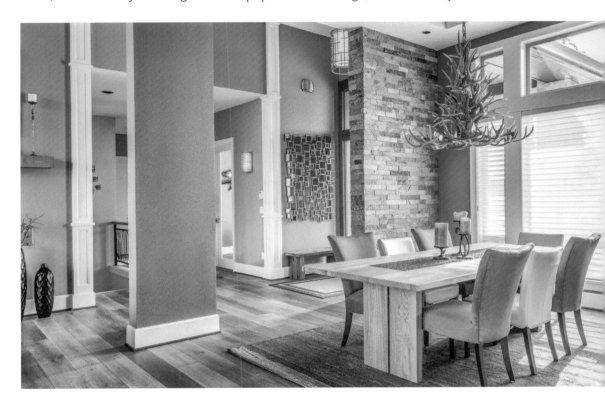

KITCHENS FOR MAVERICKS

Being comfortable while they cook is important to Mavericks, and they want anyone hanging out in their kitchen with them to feel comfortable as well. There can be more comfy backed, upholstered chairs in Maverick kitchens than in those of any other PlaceType. Flooring should be made out of materials that allow standing for a long time to be comfortable. Some glass-fronted cabinets should be installed to make it easy for Mavericks and their guests to find needed items. Mavericks' kitchens may need professional grade appliances so that they can cook the large amounts of food sometimes needed for guests. Warm colors on the walls make it more likely that Mavericks' guests will have a hearty appetite and eat all the food that's been prepared for them.

If you're a Maverick like Melissa, your kitchen should have an eat-in table, if possible. The table can be in addition to an island if the kitchen is large and an island is needed to keep the space from being cavernous. Whatever the seating arrangement, Maverick kitchens should be a comfortable space to hang out so guests keep the cook company and don't ever feel motivated to rush through a meal. Eating together is a powerful unifying social force.

Pets are important parts of Maverick homes, and they should dine and sleep in comfort, just as their owners do. Cat litter boxes can be placed in cabinets created just for them.

OFFICES/STUDIES FOR MAVERICKS

Mavericks' offices can easily become too visually complex for them to work effectively. They often have lots of objects in view because they have a sentimental link to them or haven't put them away after use, but too much going on visually leads to stress, and that harms professional performance.

Mavericks can place display shelving behind their desk chair so that they see valued objects as they enter the room and get a psychological boost, but not while they are working. Not only should most cherished objects in the office find a home out of view, but most photographs should also be placed out of a Maverick's line of sight (including peripheral vision) while they work. A few objects and photos can be in view, but no more than a half dozen items total should be on display. The objects and photos in the Maverick's view should be the ones that send the most important messages about who they are as a person—family guy, successful banker, or something else.

If you're a Maverick, make sure your office has a bulletin board, a white board, or something similar—they'll help you keep your leisure and professional activities effectively meshed. Mavericks, use a cool light bulb in your office so you feel more alert. Since Mavericks live a more balanced life than some PlaceTypes, their office may double as a hobby or craft space. Separate work surfaces, for example, one for work and one for crafts, should be installed if possible to help make this multiuse space more comfortable.

RETREATS FOR MAVERICKS—AT-HOME SPAS AND BEDROOMS

Mavericks enjoy staying in contact with their world. Telephone stands that allow hands-free talking while Mavericks shave or apply cosmetics can be installed in Maverick bathrooms along with waterproof audio and cable TV systems.

If you're a Maverick like Melissa, consider adding amenities such as a towel warmer to your bathroom—they can help put you in just the right mood to begin or end your day. Warm soaks can help you relax. Mavericks relish spending time in an outdoor Jacuzzi. Adding one creates another place to socialize.

Mavericks' bathrooms should have lots of mirrors and highly polished surfaces as well as showers that have multiple settings—from rain to massage. Unusual, intricate design is a hit with Mavericks wherever it's found. Mavericks revel in having a friend who's an expert at putting in mosaics, for example. Complex tile work is a great addition to Maverick master bathrooms, and the patterns can prevent these rooms from ever becoming dull. The tile is most effective when it's in muted shades of colors that blend with relaxing shades on the walls. Mosaics with metallic and brightly colored squares can help Mavericks create the sort of atmosphere they relish in a front hall but are just too energizing for a bathroom.

Mavericks like to get ready for the day or for a party with others, so bathrooms that are large enough for two can be desirable. Placing the toilet in a separate room off the main bathroom and shower area therefore works well for Mavericks.

Mavericks' bedrooms are not generally the private enclaves that they are for other PlaceTypes; Mavericks will bring friends to their rooms to take a look at a painting or a new pair of shoes, for example. Therefore, there need to be plenty of comfortable places to sit in that bedroom besides the bed—not everyone is *that* close a friend.

Bedrooms for Mavericks must be extremely relaxing when the Mavericks do get some alone time. To make sure that they can rest, Mavericks should keep televisions and work desks out of their bedrooms. The space should be suffused with golden light and relaxing scents. Ample organized storage is an important way for Mavericks to keep tension inducing clutter to a minimum.

Mavericks are not matchy-matchy types. If you're a Maverick, don't feel compelled to make sure that the lamps on tables on either side of your bed match, or even that the bedside tables have the same design. As long as the basic color schemes, sizes, and shapes of the setups on either side of your bed are in agreement, the space will work for you. The colors that Mavericks use in their bedrooms should be moderately bright and moderately saturated, for example, sky blue.

It may be hard to find any spaces to be alone in Mavericks' homes, but each member of the household must have a place where they can retreat—if it's not a bedroom, it may be a bench in the garden or a rock on a nearby beach. A canopy bed can be a great in-bedroom retreat, particularly if it has side curtains. Mavericks' homes need to work hard—they need to support Mavericks' active social lives as well as help them maintain their mental equilibrium.

Dynamos

MEET A DYNAMO

Cozy sorts of places that support social bonding please Dynamos. David, like other Dynamos, should create spaces that are rich in decorative details and sensory experiences. Mavericks are intensely social but always are looking for the new and different; Dynamos are just as social but choose more established traditions for their houses and offices. Dynamos are interested in making sure that the people in their homes are completely comfortable and relaxed. Even if they live in a mansion, their home feels like a vacation cottage.

Dynamos are challenged by creating a space to socialize with friends and family members in an era where everyone works outside the home and has many commitments. David and other Dynamos should purchase furniture that is curvy and comfy. Dynamos won't be drawn to whatever the next comfortable living trend may be.

If you're a Dynamo, you should live in the same neighborhood as your family and friends or as close to them as you can get. If you have to move away from the people who are important in your life, say because of a job transfer, make sure to relocate to a cohesive neighborhood with residents roughly in the same life stage as you are. If you have kids, move into an area with lots of children; if you're retired, opt for a community where many other people are retired. Also, a neighborhood with lots of pubs and coffee shops where locals actually get to know each other, is a great choice for Dynamos.

BEFORE YOU EVEN GET INSIDE

Dynamos dream of living in a home with a classic front porch stocked with wicker furniture, or at least a lobby with comfortable furniture where people may occasionally linger.

LIVING ROOMS/FAMILY ROOMS FOR DYNAMOS

Dynamos should create living rooms where people can sit comfortably for long periods of time. They are partial to sofas and should endeavor to add as many of them (and loveseats) to their living rooms as possible. Dynamos like David can even find themselves adding recliners to their living rooms. Recliners in living rooms are hard to pull off, and it's important for Dynamos to choose from current looks and not select recliners that look like they've spent many years in Granddad's basement.

Even though Dynamo living rooms are very relaxed, the room shouldn't lack for style. This is the sort of home where classic pieces of furniture such as grandfather clocks and benches in hallways are at home.

If you're a Dynamo, you don't feel compelled to be surrounded yourself with only natural materials; you can use manmade fibers and materials and even metals in your living room. To keep feeling good about your home, make sure they're easy to clean. Like Mavericks, Dynamos don't feel the need to invest in furniture that can be expected to last from one generation to the next, but furnishings in any home need to look clean and well-kept—anything else is bad for a home owner's morale, as well as their reputation.

Dynamo living rooms should have moldings at the tops and bottoms of walls and around door openings as well—the same goes for the openings in fireplaces. If possible, doorways and the like should be arches, not squared off. Art on display should be realistic depictions of landscapes or people—no purple cows here.

If you're a Dynamo, you really want your home to be a great place to hang out, and that may mean doing things like adding a satellite kitchen in a family room and lighting gathering spaces with recessed lighting on dimmers to make a space feel more intimate.

DINING ROOMS FOR DYNAMOS

Relaxed and familiar are the watchwords for Dynamo dining room design. Tables should be large enough to accommodate family and friends, and all will feel welcomed by their curved legs and edges. If you're a Dynamo, the sort of graceful furniture that could be found in an English country home will set your heart aflutter. Textiles should feature tried-and-true prints, and patterns used in a room should match or have color and design elements in common. Floors can be carpeted with patterned coverings that would look at home at Ethan Allan. Design Within Reach (a popular furniture vendor with a significant web presence) gives Dynamos migraines, although Intellectuals love much of what they find there.

Centerpieces and intentionally planned groupings of things in Dynamo homes need to be coherent and tell a consistent story—for example, this person (or family) is a world traveler, an avid fisherman, or family-focused. This message consistency makes both Dynamos and their guests comfortable immediately.

The dining rooms of Dynamos should include something such as an assortment of curvy-leafed plants (either real or realistically plastic), that will lower the stress levels of PlaceTypes who are more easily overwhelmed by visual complexity. Dynamos can have many pieces of "apparatus" such as teapots and pieces of silver. Built-in cabinets and cupboards can make storage more efficient and minimize the amount of floor space it consumes. Only a few items should be visible through transparent panels at any time. The visible assortment should take up only a couple of square feet of shelf space.

Add curvy luxurious chair rails to your dining room if you're a Dynamo. Creating upper and lower sections on your walls will give you the opportunity to include an additional wallpaper in the room.

KITCHENS FOR DYNAMOS

Dynamos have many of the same kitchen design needs as Mavericks. It is important that Dynamo kitchens be anchored by an island where guests and family members can talk with the cook as they work. This island can double as a place to eat, but its most important function is as a social hub. The island needs to be equipped with upholstered bar stools with backs, and the lighting for the island must not create glare in the eyes of seated people.

OFFICES/STUDIES FOR DYNAMOS

Dynamos should replicate in their home the aspects of their onsite offices that enhance their performance. If you're a Dynamo, try to source the same chair for your home office that you use at your workplace. The same goes for any sort of paper management trays, cord management systems, and task lighting that's in your onsite office. Even if a Dynamo's out-of-the-house office doesn't have an on-desk task light, their home office should.

Offices for Dynamos should be visually and acoustically isolated from places where people may be socializing and should be the clear territory of the person who will work there. The space needs to be free of distractions, although it is unwise to try to create a perfectly silent space. Too little stimulation is just as unnerving to people as too much. A Dynamo can benefit from adding white noise like static to their home office that's (ideally) found in their workplace as well.

Dynamos need to be able to set the temperature of their offices as well as determine lighting levels—some lights here shouldn't be integrated into a master lighting system. It's important that the offices for Dynamos be daylit and that the colors used on the walls and other surfaces be light and not very saturated. Views of nature or a fountain through the office windows, or an in-office fish tank or desktop fountain, support Dynamo knowledge work.

RETREATS FOR DYNAMOS—AT-HOME SPAS AND BEDROOMS

If you're a Dynamo, position shelves or something similar in your bathroom so you can organize your favorite lotions and potions right in the open, where you and your guests can see and relish them—but make sure not to go overboard with the number on display. Same goes for your sponges and brushes.

Dynamos, use shots of saturated but not very bright jewel tones in your towels, rugs, and curtains. Lush towels and rugs make the sensory experience in your bathroom even more intense. If you have a shower door, it can be intricately etched. If your bathroom has a shower curtain instead of a shower door, don't pass up the opportunity to coordinate it with the high-impact style of this room. Dynamo bathrooms call for art that coordinates with the overall color scheme. If you're an art connoisseur, the idea of coordinating décor and art is probably appalling, but in Dynamo bathrooms the art is not fine and should be used to support an upbeat mood.

Dynamos' bedrooms are refuges from the other people who may be in the home at any time. If you're a Dynamo, a colorful quilt is a great focal point for your bedroom. Rugs, upholstery, and curtains should match one of the less saturated colors in the quilt. Curtains should be lighter than the floor, just like the walls. For Dynamos, if the major surfaces in your bedroom are monochromatic shades of the same color, it will help your bedroom look coordinated but not be so stimulating that it's hard to relax there.

Dynamos' bedrooms shouldn't skimp on mirrors. All are welcome additions to Dynamo bedrooms. Keep the mirrors round or oval and the frames matched to the shapes of the mirrors for best results. Add baskets for storage to your bedroom; if you're a Dynamo, bringing these relaxed wicker friends into the bedroom to keep stray objects coordinated is a good idea. Again, organic forms carry the day.

Dynamos are supported by homes where both their social and private selves can live well.

CHAPTER 8

MAESTROS AND MAVENS—SPACES FOR WIZARDS

Maestros and Mavens flourish in homes where the design is edited to a soothing, sublime perfection. Their homes are best filled with curvilinear surfaces that welcome and bolster residents. Wizards accept many aspects of their environments as givens and are not likely to change them, except those related to their dominant sense.

Maestros and Mavens prefer spaces that are restrained and generally relaxing. They place a lot of importance on having a place within each home for each individual resident—an area where that person has complete control. In Wizard's homes, socializing with others is not a high priority, but thoughtful activities are.

- If you're a Wizard, you should live in homes where spaces for different functions are clearly separated from each other by walls and doors. Open-plan layouts don't go over well with Wizards.

- Wizard homes need to be filled with light, not very saturated colors, i.e., traditional pastels with a grayish tint. It is particularly important that these colors be used on the walls in Wizards' homes so that rooms seem as large as possible. If a particular room is too large to be cozy and coziness is desired in the space because it's a bedroom, a slightly darker shade can be used, but the darker color should not be more saturated than the other wall colors.

- Add mood boosting sensory elements to your home if you're a Wizard, but in moderation, as described in Chapter 2. Wizards need to be particularly attentive to their dominant sense and should not overload it. If you're a Wizard and your dominant sense is smell, for instance, and you think that you've used enough different scents in your home, you have, regardless of what others might say. Similarly, when a touch dominant Wizard feels that one more texture would be too many, or that the texture on a bedspread or rug is too much for comfort, it is.

- Wizards should live in homes, whether apartments or houses, with lots of natural light. Windows are important in Wizards' gathering spaces and bedrooms. These windows need view and light-blocking curtains to keep light out while the Wizards are sleeping and to give Wizards privacy when they need it. Since natural light is important to Wizards, they should add skylights if at all possible to rooms where they'll hang out with family and friends. Light tubes, which bring in daylight through metal conduits that snake down from openings higher on the house, are a good substitute if skylights are impossible.

- Visible dirt and wear on surfaces in their homes are not very distressing to Wizards but can be tough on visitors. The use of materials that will stain or weather unattractively should be minimized, and cabinet and appliance finishes that show dirt or fingerprints should be avoided. It should be hard to make chosen flooring materials look dirty, so ceramic floor tiles are out because dirt can accumulate in the spaces between the tiles, but textured rugs are in; ditto for ceramic tile on countertops and textured countertops. Patterns on surfaces can be good, because they hide dirt. It's harder to pick out a dirty spot on a marble surface than on a single color laminate. Darker colors on countertops and floors should be selected along with upholstery that coordinates with pet colors so as to make pet hair less visible. The need for visible cleanliness when others come by means that an investment in ultra-efficient vacuum cleaners and washing machines is money well spent, if you're a Wizard. The best way for Wizards to deal with wear and grime may be to replace furnishings after scrubbing and vacuuming stop being effective at sprucing them up. This line of reasoning should lead Wizards to buy less expensive furniture, as well as rugs, pots, pans, and a host of other things that inevitably do become dirty.

- Though they will travel to the homes of friends and family members as desired, Wizards don't need to live in their midst. Wizards should choose to reside in a centrally located place with ready access to modern conveniences such as grocery stores and casual restaurants. They do best when living in a space where they are well buffered from their neighbors, either by thick, acoustically impermeable walls or lawns. Wizards should also live in homes with views of nature or lots of art depicting nature. For nature views, suburbs are often good homes for Wizards.

Maestros

MEET A MAESTRO

Maestros prefer spaces that are edited to a sublime, distinctive perfection where individuals can enrich their souls. They should live in environments filled with carefully selected objects. Color palettes here are soothing light shades, and patterns in upholstery are unusual. If patterns are present, use colors near each other on the color wheel (blues and greens, for example).

- All of the rooms in the Maestro home should be designed to be relatively relaxing, whether they're public, private, meditation spaces, or dining areas.

- It's important that some areas are set aside as private spaces that are clearly owned by a specific person. If a Maestro has for some reason purchased an open-plan home, screens should be carefully positioned to divide up the open space if actual walls can't be added. If walls aren't a viable option, Maestros like Margaret have other options to divide up a large space: painting different areas slightly different colors, while keeping the tones light and unsaturated; lowering the ceiling in part of the space; or changing flooring or carpeting between areas. Within each of these mini-rooms, furniture needs to be grouped so that at least a few of the people in the space can sit with a view out over the entire area from a space where they feel "protected"—designing for secure views over nearby areas as discussed in Chapter 2 is very important here.

- Spaces in Maestro homes should feature a fleet of comfortable single-person chairs and maybe a loveseat. Sofas are not good selections for public spaces, although they can be used in private areas for reclining while reading, napping, or watching TV alone.

BEFORE YOU EVEN GET INSIDE

Maestro homes can have a sign at the front door with the names of the adults who live there clearly printed. Its design should mesh with the look and colors of the house. The front steps of a Maestro home should also be lit with a warm, golden light from a simple outdoor fixture that welcomes guests and residents. Foot mats should be positioned to minimize the amount of dirt tracked into the home.

FLOOR PLANS FOR MAESTROS

Floor plans favored by Maestros have oodles of spaces that are claimed by individuals, but unusual is good—turrets are terrific! These watchtower spaces are particularly desirable if they are high enough off the ground to be nestled in leafy tree branches like a fabulous tree house with views up and down the block or over nearby meadows. Spaces with a view out over private outdoor spaces, such as gardens or water features are also desirable for Maestros. The easier it is to fall into daydreaming while looking out the window, the better.

LIVING ROOMS/FAMILY ROOMS FOR MAESTROS

The walls in Maestro living rooms should be painted warm colors that are relatively bright but not very saturated. This color scheme will help the space seem larger and smooth social interactions as described in Chapter 2. A collection of these types of colors should be used in the upholstery as well as the walls, and any patterns present in rugs, wallpaper, or upholstery need to be subtle and small in scale.

Coffee tables and end tables should be significant; none of the clear Lucite trays with the insubstantial legs here. The sorts of end tables and coffee tables preferred by Maestros are large in scale, sometimes big enough so that they're described as "sturdy," and are made out of materials such as wood or metal. Maestros furnishing their homes carefully consider unusual pieces of furniture and purchase those that align with their budget.

Maestros can purchase art that is abstract and/or modern. When themes in the art can be identified, the most prized pieces are likely to be landscapes or linked to nature. The works selected should be filled with curving lines and be low on straight lines and sharp angles. Tabletop sculptures in unusual materials, perhaps used in unlikely combinations, are good choices as long as they meet the "curvy" mandate. Lighting in Maestro living rooms should be from lamps that individuals can turn on and off at will and should have bulbs that cast warm, golden-toned light.

A fireplace is really important in a Maestro living room, but it can take an unconventional form. Maestros can gather around a traditional hearth with brick and wooden surround, a potbelly stove that allows a tiny view through its grate to the flames inside, or they may choose something else. Anything goes with the Maestros' fire.

DINING ROOMS FOR MAESTROS

Maestro dining rooms should contain a mix of seats, some with arms, some without. Chairs should have cushioned seats and backs. They should be arranged around a rectangular table and, whenever possible, should be lit by candles instead of by overhead light. All electrical lighting in the room should be dimmable, and the best chandelier for above the table will be a simple, classic design with curved arms. Furniture should be made of wood.

Walls in the dining room should be a warm color that is not very saturated but relatively bright. A single pattern can be used in the room, which must coordinate with this color. This pattern might be on upholstery, walls, or the floor. All other surfaces should be shades of that warm color. The dining room should have doors that can close so pets can be kept out of the area as desired.

KITCHENS FOR MAESTROS

Maestro kitchens should feature innovative materials and finishes that preserve the materials' inherent integrity. Stone surfaces are unlikely to have shiny finishes, and terra cotta floors won't either. Maestros are not interested in do-it-yourself projects and are not necessarily ambitious cooks, so kitchens are not asked to do much heavy lifting, in contrast to Catalysts' kitchens, and high performance appliances are not needed. Appliances should have matte finishes. Warm colors in pastels of moderate saturation and brightness should be featured in Maestros' kitchens.

Cabinets with solid doors (and no windows) that feature varnished wood are good choices for Maestros. The cabinets should be relatively plain, although they can have curved hardware. Butcher-block sections of counter top can be installed—they provide another opportunity to integrate wood with visible grain into the kitchen.

Ventilation hoods are important to Maestros because they eliminate smells. The hood should have a gently curving shape that softens the somewhat austere feel of this kitchen. An interior herb garden arranged on glass shelves in a sunny kitchen window can to some extent clean the air while adding a few comforting curves to the kitchen, as well as providing fresh herbs for meals.

Islands in Maestro kitchens are strictly work centers, not places to hang out with friends and family. They can be eliminated altogether if the kitchen has adequate counter space without them. Maestros feel more comfortable in kitchens where tools and countertop appliances are all packed away into drawers and cabinets.

OFFICES/STUDIES FOR MAESTROS

Offices for Maestros are minimalist spaces; only a few personalizing photos and souvenirs should be placed around the area. Office supplies should be carefully stowed in drawers, and whiteboards or corkboards need to be carefully pruned and clearly managed. Storage should have doors that don't allow what's being stored to be seen. Maestros need to be particularly attuned to eradicating visual clutter in their midst.

Functionality and efficiency are important in Maestro offices. Needed tools are available, but none that are superfluous are present, and all should fit into cabinets and drawers. Maestros should own—and use—ergonomic chairs, footrests, and wrist rests. Their desks should be adjustable to both the proper sitting and standing height.

Maestros' offices should be suffused with golden light, i.e., warm bulbs should be used throughout. Daylight should stream into the space from windows, skylights, and/or clerestory windows. If Maestros' offices don't have a view of nature, they must have photos and paintings of landscapes on the walls; otherwise, a water feature needs to be available either inside or outside.

RETREATS FOR MAESTROS—AT-HOME SPAS AND BEDROOMS

When creating bathrooms, Maestros need to make sure that they do not sacrifice ergonomics and basic human comfort (think glare, temperature, and similar concerns) in their quest for uniqueness. Bathrooms with windows are best for Maestros—not only can a window be opened to clear out steam and prevent mold, but if no neighboring homes hover too closely, its curtains can be opened during long meditative soaks to make the experience that much more restorative, particularly if there's a nature view. Skylights can be used to incorporate natural light into the space.

Maestros welcome modern evolutions of the classic white bathroom. Near whites are a great bathroom color choice for Maestros, because many surfaces in these colors are actually easy to clean, or to deep clean, if necessary. To keep their spaces from becoming too stereotypical to please them, Maestros should consider options such as using tiles and surfaces that are opalescent.

When Maestros like Melissa are in their bedrooms, they need to be in an oasis of comfort. Fuzzy, soft bed linens and upholstery are good selections. For example, flannels or similar materials can be used throughout the space. When pets are present, fabrics that are difficult to shred and nearly indestructible are good choices.

Large solid blocks of color on the bed or walls are welcome in Maestro bedrooms. Subtle, small-scale patterns on rugs and other large surfaces will keep the space from being too monotonous. It's desirable for Maestros living in homes with others to have a comfortable seating area in their bedrooms where they can retreat and read, write, and so on without being interrupted or needing to justify their activity. Two Maestro spouses need two such spaces in their home, and if a Maestro lives with a partner who's not a Maestro, the non-Maestro needs to respect the in-bedroom territory.

The furniture in Maestro bedrooms should be relatively more curvilinear than rectilinear in appearance—which means beds and bureaus with curved headboards and legs, for example. Some of that curvilinear furniture should provide enough storage space for all of those socks, underpants, and sweaters that make a room look cluttered when they're out on display. The sentimental items that Maestros choose to surround themselves with should be limited by "rules" allowing them to be placed only in small display spaces, such as trim wall hung shelves with limited capacity.

The in-bedroom TV must be able to disappear in a Maestro bedroom. This can happen in a variety of ways, from an armoire to a case with doors that can be closed in front of a wall-mounted television set. A set that retracts into the footboard of a bed is pretty slick but can also be expensive. An in-bedroom sound system can play music or nature audio tracks that can help Maestros relax and sleep.

Maestros' homes are havens, refuges where they can recover from stresses encountered outside the house, and safe harbors from which they can sail again into the wide, wild world.

Mavens

MEET A MAVEN

Mike is a Maven. In spaces that support Mike and other Mavens, established design prevails in an unobtrusive way that sustains as it contributes to individual experiences. Mavens' homes should feature art such as classic, realistic landscapes. Their furnishings need elegant classic lines like those found in a camelback sofa. Bentwood furniture, with its clean curved lines, also meshes with the Maven PlaceType.

Restorative exterior nature views are really important to Mavens, but if they aren't feasible, interior plants, real or artificial, will do, as will tabletop water features. Interior plants are so important to Mavens that it's worth their while to set up in-home planters and to try to remember to keep them alive.

Mavens live their best lives in spaces that are functional and directly support the activities they enjoy. Before Mavens begin to design their homes, they need to carefully review how their home can contribute to positive living. Symmetry, balance, and harmony are divinities worshipped by Mavens, and the design of their homes and the objects in it should reflect this devotion.

BEFORE YOU EVEN GET INSIDE

Mike, like most Mavens, enjoys welcoming his friends to his home and he wants to make sure they have a top-notch experience that begins when they get out of their car. The door should always be freshly painted and the hardware polished.

LIVING ROOMS/FAMILY ROOMS FOR MAVENS

Mavens must take care to ensure that their living rooms and family rooms reflect the common interests and values of both children and parents and that their guests feel comfortable there. These spaces need to provide comfortable seats for groups of the sizes that can be expected to visit.

Mavens feel best when sofas are few and far between and individual chairs are the most plentiful seating option. Seats should be arranged so that they are interspersed with substantial end tables and coffee tables. All tables should be constructed from traditional materials such as wood. For Mavens to feel comfortable, their living room or family room must be clearly separated, ideally by walls, from the rest of the rooms in their home. Focal colors in the living room and/or family room should be not very saturated but fairly bright, such as light blue-grays and pale sandy browns.

Seats can all be oriented toward a classic, clean-lined fireplace, large window, or other focal point in a loosely configured circle. The focal point that makes the most sense will be tied to the Maven's interests and talents—it might be a sculpture they have purchased or created themselves, an exquisite fish tank, a small mountain of luscious green plants, or a wonderful bouquet of seasonal flowers. This focal point must be a reasonable place for people to rest their eyes when conversation lags. If possible, the ceiling should be lowered over the main conversation area in a Maven's living room to make the space seem more comfortable and welcoming.

Mavens' living rooms should not feature moldings at the tops or bottoms of walls or around doorways or windows. Similarly, light fixtures should be simple shells that lie nearly flat against the ceiling or are recessed.

If you're a Maven like Mike, you should actively design for each of your senses. This could include adding a sound system that coordinates music in each room and relaxing scents such as vanilla and lavender (see Chapter 2 for information on other scents) to the space. Mavens should select carpets and upholstery fabrics that feel soft against the skin. Zones for lights, heating, and air-conditioning should be created in a Maven's living rooms and throughout their homes so that people can move as needed to enhance either social situations (warmer and a little dimmer) or intellectual work (cooler and a little brighter).

DINING ROOMS FOR MAVENS

Maven dining rooms should follow the same basic design rules as those for Maestros. Rectangular tables, for example, are also best in Maven's homes. Dining chairs can have arms and can be extremely comfortable places to sit; it is paramount that a table large enough for expected groups be placed in the dining room. Mavens should make sure that their homes do have a separate room for dining. If this is not possible, the dining "room" must be clearly delineated using wall paint colors, flooring changes, etc.

KITCHENS FOR MAVENS

Mavens' quest for minimalistic functionality is clearest in their kitchens. The tools required to cook as Mavens desire should be present, but nothing tacked on "for show." For example, if a Maven enjoys making pastries, a portion of the countertop should definitely be marble, but if the Maven is not interested in baking, no marble need be installed. Another example: if they regularly have large dinner parties, Mavens should have two dishwashers; if not, one will do just fine. If you're a Maven, you should stock your kitchen with appliances you've found useful and dependable.

Sinks that are made out of sturdy tested materials such as aluminum should be selected by Mavens. A traditional single or double tub shape is practical in the widest variety of situations. The kitchen faucet can be extendable and provide a variety of spray options. A backsplash that is a simple extension of the countertop material is suggested because it has the clean silhouette that Mavens prefer and is also easy to clean. Simple wooden cabinets with doors that block views into the cabinets are also suggested.

Mavens shouldn't deviate from efficient "kitchen triangle" arrangements—kitchen-based socializing is much less important than efficient food production. If you're a Maven, you can make your kitchen island the focal point of your kitchen. A multi-height island that can be used in several ways, say for homework, eating, and standing work, is a good option for Mavens. Track lighting is similarly suggested for Mavens' kitchens.

Homes in which Mavens thrive feature workspaces from which the home is managed and separate spots where professional work is done. The kitchen can feature a clearly defined and well-appointed desk area to keep important home management tasks clearly on track.

OFFICES/STUDIES FOR MAVENS

At-home offices for Mavens should be dedicated to working from home—they shouldn't double as home schoolrooms or have some other function. Maven offices must be free of distractions and filled with natural light. The walls should also be painted in unsaturated but bright greens. Sitting and standing work surfaces should be provided. Mavens must be able to control the light levels and temperatures in the space. Green leafy plants, natural light, and views of nature or water (natural or manmade) are important in Maven offices. Maintaining moderate visual complexity via effective storage is important. So is the ability to work free of audio and visual distractions.

RETREATS FOR MAVENS—AT-HOME SPAS AND BEDROOMS

Mavens' bathrooms should have large amounts of built-in storage to accommodate many relatively small objects.

If you're a Maven, you should install white, tiled, traditional bathrooms—it's clear when they're clean, and they have a classic look. Appropriately colored stone should be used when possible, and small black and white octagonal tiles are a good choice for the floor.

Oval bathtubs are better choices for Mavens' bathrooms than rectilinear ones, and the same goes for sinks. Glass shower enclosures win out over shower curtains in Mavens' bathrooms. Taps should be curvy and shower curtains (if any) crisp. Floating vanities (cabinets without legs that are firmly attached to the wall) make it easier to clean bathroom floors and are positively viewed by Mavens. The whole floating vanity must appear light, with a thin, apparently lightweight counter. Flowers can play a starring role in Mavens' bathrooms. Dried or fresh, they should be the visual highlights of these bathrooms; dried lavender still on the stem is a good choice for larger containers.

Mavens need retreats in their bedrooms; these are areas where they can really relax. Window seats are great places for Mavens to ponder their worlds. If all else fails, add a high-backed chair and ottoman to your bedroom and orient it toward the window.

Mavens' bedrooms need to be very simple visually, so closet management and providing storage wherever possible in the bedroom is important. Ottomans, window seats, and the space under the bed should all be used by Mavens to keep the visual complexity down in their bedroom. Bedside tables whose tops lift like those on toy chests to reveal large storage spaces can work well here. If something's in a Maven's bedroom, there has to be a place to stash it from which it can be retrieved without damage or stress.

Successful Maven bedrooms are sparingly furnished and contain only a few photographs, pieces of artwork, or other personally meaningful objects. The few items present need to be extremely important to the owner of the space. Linens and draperies need to mesh with a well-established but relatively minimalist look.

Walls, floors, upholstery, and bedspreads should be in a monochromatic color scheme that's not whites and beiges. All should be light colors that aren't very saturated. Blue shades are best. Lighting should be golden and adjustable to be dim enough for intimate conversations, in person or over the phone, and bright enough for reading.

Mavens work hard, and they are most successful when their homes do, as well.

CHAPTER 9

CREATING A PLACE THAT MORE CAN ENJOY

When people live alone, one primary PlaceType can be supported through design. The situation changes when a couple or a group, family or otherwise, shares a home. Design discussions may become heated when more than one PlaceType is involved, but it is possible to create a home where multiple PlaceTypes thrive.

Only homes are discussed in this chapter, because offices can contain many PlaceTypes and employee groups can change quickly. To design offices beyond a single person's work area, the material included in Chapter 2 related to concentration and socializing with others should be applied without concern for PlaceType.

You can determine your own PlaceType by answering the questions posed in Chapter 3. People with whom you share a space can also answer those questions, or, if they are not available to take the personality quiz directly, you can take it for them by selecting the quiz responses that seem to best describe them.

Consider the Bennett family. Betsy is an Adventurer and Brian is a Maven. Betsy loves to reinvent their space as new needs arise and new design opportunities come to mind. Brian is all for the status quo. Brian is often simply overwhelmed by Betsy's decorating plans that pulse with multiple colors and oodles of textures. Shine is Betsy's friend but makes Brian's head hurt. After reading the descriptions of PlaceTypes in this book, you can no doubt anticipate many of their other design-related conflicts.

The spaces in any home can be divided into "my places" and "our places." My places "belong" mainly to a single individual, while our places are shared. My places should support the PlaceType of their primary user; others can go back to their own areas when being "out of place" gets to be too much. Each resident (after toddlerhood) must have control over a space in the home whose design supports their PlaceType. It is desirable to have multiple places that support each of the PlaceTypes sharing a house whenever possible, so that individuals can choose from among several options where they can comfortably spend time. This spot will generally align with that person's territory in the home. Betsy's "my place" is the sitting room off the master bedroom, and Brian's is his home office in the attic. In this example, we're discussing the experiences of two people who live in a home, but the same principles apply when larger groups share a living space.

But what about "our places"? The "our" spaces of a home may include the entryway, living room, family room, dining room, kitchen, master bedroom, and master bath; they're generally more public spaces. Often a home office or study clearly belongs to one person, but that is not necessarily true. "Our places" need to be carefully designed to make each of the people living in a home as comfortable as possible in that space. We will review an assortment of potential sharing related issues in the paragraphs that follow.

The most important home design issue stressing Brian and Betsy's relationship is their different sources of energy. Betsy's is from outside herself, while the reverse is true for Brian. This is also the most important difference that can arise between any two PlaceTypes, and it must be resolved before any others are addressed. When Adventurers, Guardians, Mavericks, or Dynamos live with Investigators, Sages, Maestros, or Mavens, each partner needs to make some important changes in their expectations about their home. The first set of PlaceTypes was categorized as more extraverted when completing the Place-Personality assessment guide in Chapter 3, while the latter set of PlaceTypes was more introverted.

When Adventurers, Guardians, Mavericks, or Dynamos share a home with Investigators, Sages, Maestros, or Mavens, the first order of business is to develop shared public spaces such as living rooms, family rooms, and dining rooms. If these areas are all one open-plan area, they should remain that way. If they are not, they can be converted to open plan if possible. As an example, if entire walls can't be removed, then large windows can be broken through from one of the public rooms to the next. If for some reason it is not possible to open up the space, then it needs to be designed to support the more extraverted Adventurers, Guardians, Mavericks, and Dynamos. If a space is already open plan or becomes so, all additional design decisions must support the more introverted Investigator, Sage, Maestro, and Maven PlaceTypes. Taking these measures means that the design should then work for their PlaceTypes.

First, the space needs to be visually divided into sections that correspond to each of the different functions of the space: hanging out with friends, dining, cooking, etc. These areas can be distinguished by using different shades of the same color paint on their walls, ceilings of different heights, different rugs, pools of light from lighting fixtures—whatever is feasible in the space. Lightweight moveable screens approximately six or seven feet tall should be brought into the space as seating areas need to be established in the living and dining areas. This means that seats are arranged roughly in an inward facing circle. A focal element that can capture and hold people's attention should be in the center of each circle—this might be a freestanding fireplace, a sculpture, or a fish tank. The screens should be positioned so that people sitting in some of the chairs in each functional area do not have a good view of people sitting in the other functional areas. Investigators, Sages, Maestros, and Mavens should sit in these vision-blocked seats. Some chairs on pivot mechanisms can be placed near windows, and when just the owners are present, the more introverted partner can sit in these seats and pivot so that they are looking out of the windows.

It is important that any modifications made to the public spaces do not restrict daylight from flowing into it. Also, all public spaces must be a comfortable temperature year-round, and ventilation (movement of air) in the entire space must be acceptable to the people living in the home.

Bedrooms and bathrooms are private areas of the home where Adventurers, Guardians, Mavericks, and Dynamos may have design-related clashes with Investigators, Sages, Maestros, and Mavens. Bedrooms should be designed to support the Investigator, Sage, Maestro, and Maven PlaceTypes, while bathrooms should be consistent with the needs of Adventurers, Guardians, Mavericks, and Dynamos.

People who were categorized as relatively more conscientious on the PlaceType assessment guide may find themselves living with people who are less conscientious.

That means Adventurers, Guardians, Investigators, and Sages may be sharing a space with Mavericks, Dynamos, Maestros, and Mavens. What should happen in this circumstance?

When Adventurers, Guardians, Investigators, and Sages (who are relatively more conscientious) live with Mavericks, Dynamos, Maestros, and Mavens (who are relatively less conscientious), it's very important that environments clearly support whatever task is planned for an area—so at least in most of the Western world, kitchens need ovens. Efficient action is important to those who are more conscientious, and kitchens, laundry rooms, and bathrooms in particular need to be developed in ways that support efficient use. High-performing environments are not as crucial to the mental well-being of people who are relatively less conscientious, but being in efficiently organized areas does not compromise their well-being. Some examples of efficient design are straightforward, such as the often discussed "kitchen triangle," which positions sinks, stoves, and refrigerators in a rough triangle. Others are more subtle. For example, having the toilet in a bathroom separated from the main body of the bathroom via floor-to-ceiling walls and a full door that closes can lead to more efficient use of bathroom sinks and mirrors.

Also, when Adventurers, Guardians, Investigators, and Sages share a home with Mavericks, Dynamos, Maestros, and Mavens, it is crucial that the environment nudges users toward being orderly and supports cleanliness. Many conveniently placed storage options that don't permit people to see their contents work well. Also, surfaces, such as countertops that don't stain easily, for example, can support apparent cleanliness in a space.

When people who are more conscientious live with people who are less conscientious, selecting furniture can become difficult, and this is the kind of situation in which people with one set of PlaceTypes may disagree with the other. In this case, furnishings selected should be relatively light in scale, which means one person could, at least theoretically, move a chair by themselves. When considering a sofa, it may be hard to apply this criterion, but it can be done. If you're trying to categorize a sofa in terms of scale, imagine that the couch is on a carpet and decide if a regular person could drag it from place to place on a single floor of a home. Some couches can be moved by a single person in this way and some cannot.

Another way to think of scale is in terms of "white space." To understand white space in this context, consider a photo of a piece of furniture, say a chair, with the piece of furniture completely filling the field of view. The top of the chair therefore aligns with the top of the frame of the picture, the two arms align with the left and right sides of the image, and the bottom of the chair's feet with the bottom edge of the photo. (It may be impossible to actually take this photo because of the relative height and length of a chair, but for the sake of this mental exercise, imagine that it is indeed possible.) White space is the area around the elements of furniture photographed, the chair in this case. Pieces of furniture with a lighter scale have more white space and those that are heavier have less. A graceful and somewhat delicate bentwood rocking chair is very light scale, while a traditional recliner, the sort that the father in a 1950s sitcom would find himself in each evening after dinner, is much heavier in scale.

When Adventurers, Guardians, Investigators, and Sages live with Mavericks, Dynamos, Maestros, and Mavens, the furniture should be relatively light in scale but be relatively curvilinear in form in all areas of the home, public and private. This means that the more conscientious types are able to reposition furniture in their home as desired, but the general look of the furniture will make the relatively less conscientious types feel comfortable in the space.

Some people were categorized as relatively more open to experience in the PlaceType assessment and others as relatively less open to experience. As a result, Adventurers, Investigators, Mavericks, and Maestros can find themselves living with Guardians, Dynamos, Sages, and Mavens. Diversity on this factor can lead to issues that need to be resolved throughout the home. In general, public places in the home should be designed to support those less open to new experiences, while private areas should support being more open to new experience. In Betsy and Brian's case, this means that the public areas of their home will support Betsy's PlaceType, while the bedroom and master bathroom support Brian's.

It is possible that a space can be more likely to be used by one particular person at a certain time and by another person at another time of day. In these cases, if there are design-related issues due to differences in PlaceType, it may be possible to change the form of the space in some way so that it supports one PlaceType during certain hours and another at other times. Consider a home office. People who differ on the first PlaceType factor, meaning couples who have been categorized as relatively more extraverted or introverted, can work effectively there at different times of day. For example, it might be more heavily scented and have a louder ambient soundtrack during some parts of the day than others. Also, one individual might work sitting with a view of the office that is more visually complex and features art or images with people in them, while the other is situated with a view that's simpler and that features art or images of natural landscapes.

No matter what the PlaceTypes of the people sharing a home, the personalizing items in their shared spaces should tell their joint story. Sure, there may be photos of individuals, but in these common areas there should also be pictures of the members of the family doing things together that they mutually value—for example, volunteering at a political campaign or climbing the Matterhorn—and jointly treasured objects. Adding photos and souvenirs to commonly owned spaces in a home is a way for the people living there to bond with each other.

It is important to recognize that people sharing a space may differ on physical parameters as well as psychological ones. Successful places find a way to accommodate these differences, because, if they're not acknowledged, tension will build in the home.

For example, some people are much taller than others. The taller individuals can store objects higher off the floor than the shorter ones, but will sooner feel a lowered section of ceiling is oppressively close to the floor than a shorter person will. In addition, some people are heavier than others, and there are also left-handers and right-handers who will use the same space. Each partner needs to ensure that the other is not physically stressed. This means tall people must make sure their shorter cohabitants have ready access to stable step ladders and that lighter, sturdier objects are stored on higher shelves. Shorter people in turn must make sure that dropped ceilings never make their taller friends feel uncomfortable and that there is furniture in the space for people of different heights. Also, if at all possible, all seats in a home should be able to accommodate the larger people who live there. However, antiques probably can't be retrofitted to suit all.

Just as we all differ physically, we all differ in the personal experiences we've had living in a home. This has repercussions for how a home is used and issues such as how cleaning happens. These can quickly become emotionally charged issues when the people living in a home have different related experiences. It is important for people living together to calmly discuss these sorts of issues when they set up joint housekeeping. An example: one person in a pair may believe that a kitchen is clean when all dirty dishes are in the dishwasher and refuse is in the trash can and recycling container. The other may not believe that same kitchen is clean until all dishes have been removed from that dishwasher and neatly returned to their places in cupboards and all trash and recycling containers have been emptied.

People living in a home also share a set of daily hassles, such as finding stored supplies when they are needed. Setting up a set of "operating procedures" for the home can prevent these daily hassles from becoming a major issue.

We're all individuals, and we differ in our personalities as well as life experiences. Common interests and values draw us together and make us interested in sharing a space, and the mutual goodwill we build through our common interests and shared values provides a firm foundation on which we can develop compromises so that people who have different PlaceTypes or experiences can all share a home, one that supports all of them and helps them live their desired lives.

CHAPTER 10

SPECIAL PLACE-RELATED NEEDS

There are individual differences besides PlaceType that influence the sorts of spaces in which people thrive. This chapter reviews design that enhances the lives of very young and very old people, individuals with autism, and people with Attention Deficit/ Hyperactivity Disorder (ADHD).

Young People

Children have clear place-related concerns, just as adults do. Children need comfortable levels of control over their physical experiences to the extent that is reasonable, just as adults do, although three-year-olds should have less input on the design of their bedrooms and how they can use them than fifteen-year-olds. But as soon as they can talk, kids do need to be able to express their opinions about the places they sleep and any additional territories they may have; reasonable options that children suggest should be adopted. Again, as with adults, the options available should be a carefully curated set that aligns with how kids will likely need and want to use a space. Two-year-olds need a place where they can retreat and regroup in their home, and even children as young as three years old need to have a territory and privacy when they want it. From age five on, people have a home field advantage—when other children come over to their home territory, kids over five are apt to perform better at whatever game is being played than the visiting children. Children eight to twelve years old think it's very important to have their own territory.

One-year-olds should, if possible, be able to see views of nature from their home; those who do seem to develop more quickly cognitively. Kids as young as age one play with their toys for shorter periods of time when they can hear a television, even if that television set is broadcasting a program geared toward adults. Since playing with toys can support development, it is best to separate children's play zones from television areas. Kids age three and older need to be able to restock their levels of mental energy, just as adults do. They also do best in spaces with moderate levels of visual complexity.

Research has shown that children clearly prefer particular colors. For example, young kids under five are partial to interior spaces that are red, although in general they prefer cooler colors to warmer ones. In general, children and adults have the same favorite color: blue.

Researchers have investigated differences in the colors that boys and girls seven to eleven prefer to see used in rooms. Boys go for darker and less saturated colors while girls favor brighter, more saturated hues. Girls were also more likely to prefer reds and purples than boys.

High contrast color combinations—say black and white together—are good for areas that will be used by infants and toddlers (up to age three) as these patterns support their well-being and visual development. Palettes for young children do not need to be only white and black, however. White, black, fire-engine red, and sapphire blue are readily distinguished by children at these ages.

Children generally prefer the same sorts of art as adults. Pictures with moderate visual complexity carry the day. A study of kids from age eight to fifteen found that they preferred paintings of landscapes that let viewers see into the distance of that landscape. Bad news for the aunts who diligently buy clown themed stuff for kids' rooms: clowns scare many young children, and older children can find them and cartoon characters unacceptable because "they're for babies."

Teenagers and young adults have an approach to life that differs from both children and adults because of the form of their brains. Between ages fifteen and twenty-two or so, adolescents' brains are significantly different than those of both younger and older people. Researchers have conclusively demonstrated that our brains continue to develop into our twenties and that the last parts of our brains to achieve adult form are those related to taking risks and paying attention. The design-related consequence of this late term development is that young adults take risks that adults would not. To protect people in this age range from themselves, it is a good idea to avoid if possible presenting these reckless souls with circumstances that may motivate one kid to dare another kid to do risky things. For example, make sure railings around roof decks are hard to climb over. Obviously, no home can be completely young person proofed, and generally families do plan to live in a home both before and after family members become risk-mature adults, but it is useful to develop contingency plans, remove opportunities to take chances, and so on to the extent possible in homes where young people live.

We've generally talked about creating positive spaces where people will be in good moods, but it's important to recognize that teenagers (those in the study discussed here were fourteen years old) want to be in a bad mood more frequently than people who are much older than they are. This will surprise no one who's ever been charged with parenting a fourteen-year-old. What will surprise parents is the fact that experiencing these negative moods may help adolescents become emotionally independent from adults and establish their own identify as a person. Perverse as it may sound, this research indicates it may be a good idea for parents to let their children spend time in the negative sort of atmosphere in their rooms that they seem determined to create.

Older People

Older individuals have the same design-based needs as the middle-aged, although the declining capabilities of their eyes, ears, and sense of balance mean that environments that will be used extensively by older people need to be modified. Different sorts of materials can combat both increasingly troublesome glare and echoes, for example. People begin to lose sensory capabilities at different ages, so generalizing when people should modify lighting systems in their homes and make other similar changes isn't a good idea. However, it seems likely that by about age seventy-five, most people will need to make the environmental modifications discussed in this section.

All adult humans need a territory and privacy when desired, as was discussed in Chapter 2. If older individuals lose control over their physical environment, their well-being will suffer.

As we get older, we see colors as yellower than they actually are and colors seem less vivid and bright to us. That means Kelly green begins to look more like lighter spring greens, for example, or reds look more like pinks. This leads older people in general to select whites and bright colors as their favorite colors. For older eyes, blue can be particularly difficult to see. As people age, higher saturation colors are easier to see and differentiate and are liked more than low saturation colors. Low saturation colors are generally seen as grays, and an environment containing generally low saturation colors will seem drab to older individuals. In spaces that older individuals are developing for themselves or that are being designed for their use, color palettes should be developed with these differences in perception in mind.

By the age of sixty, our eyes are blocking lots of light that we experience, requiring changes in the way spaces are lit and colors selected. For example, by your sixtieth birthday, about one third of the light that hits a twenty-year-old retina will fall onto yours, if you're both in the same space. This situation can be overcome by increasing the contrasts between colors used or changing light levels.

Recommendations for lighting for older eyes include:

- Use a range of different lights: ambient, task, and accent lights, for starters.

- Ambient light levels should be the same in all spaces lit and should shine on vertical surfaces—this not only adds light to a space but defines its edges and makes it seem larger. Older eyes find it more difficult than younger eyes to adjust to light of different intensities.

- Avoid light and dark patches on floors or similar blotches on the walls; they make it difficult to figure out what's going on in a space. Using light colors on walls and ceilings helps to reduce the shadows.

- Position lights so they illuminate areas that need to have light and so that human bodies don't block light sources and create a shadow over the space to be lit. That means lights need to be in front of the places where you can expect people to be and not behind them.

- Eliminate glare, whether it is due to artificial or natural light. Indirect lighting (which shines onto the ceiling or a wall instead of down from the ceiling toward people) can produce less glare and fewer shadows. Don't use shiny surfaces on floors, countertops, or other surfaces; work to minimize glare.

- Older people in general prefer 2,700K to 3,000K lights at home, and they function better in these lighting conditions.

There's conflicting evidence about the ability of older individuals (around age seventy-five or so) to block out visual distractions. If someone who will use a space you are developing does have trouble focusing when they're trying to pay bills or performing other such tasks, create a work niche for them. It should have simple, painted walls, and a work surface should be mounted so that people face into the niche while working.

As we age, more and more of us snore, and it can be difficult to sleep through the racket. The best solution to all that noise may just be separate rooms, particularly if they're adjoining, with a sound-insulated door connecting the two rooms directly so that moving between them does not require walking along a more public hallway. Companies developing communities for people over fifty-five are more and more frequently building homes with a separate bedroom accessed through a doorway in a master bedroom's bathroom. This also works well if people have different habits regarding late-night television viewing or iPad use. In an existing home, the easiest way to create a "snore zone" is to add a door between two bedrooms or to connect the master bedroom to another preexisting bedroom in the house by adding separate doorways into a bathroom that is located between the two rooms. Connecting the two bedrooms by way of the bathroom means that the bathroom space will provide additional sound buffering.

As people age, they often have trouble hearing. Rugs, upholstery, and curtains—all of which help reduce echoes—are desirable additions to spaces they will use. It's extremely stressful not to be able to understand conversations, so cutting echoes is important, as is making sure that the furniture in gathering places allows people with impaired hearing to easily see the mouths of people speaking; a lot of us are better lip readers than we realize. Configurations that support lip reading have all individuals seated so that they can easily make eye contact. Also, including some furniture in a space that is light enough in scale so that it can be repositioned for easy lip viewing during conversations is handy.

Hearing street noise at night has been linked to strokes, so light-blocking drapes are a good idea in the rooms of older individuals. These curtains will also block out light from outside the home while people are napping. The positive effects of sleeping in dark spaces were discussed in Chapter 2.

Older people may have issues with tripping and slipping. Ergonomics texts provide detailed information on eliminating these household hazards. If an older individual is living with younger ones, it is important that common workspaces, such as the kitchen have lighting levels and so on that support the older person, as should at least some of the common areas in the home where people sit together to talk.

People with Autism Spectrum Disorder

Autism is a complex disease that can take many different forms, so it is often referred to as autism spectrum disorder. People with autism can be either oversensitive or undersensitive (aka "hyposensitive") to sensations they experience. An autistic person who is oversensitive (or hypersensitive) to sounds, for example, can be distressed by noises that seem quite acceptable to other people, while other autistic individuals are hyposensitive to sound, which means that person does not respond to very loud sounds as other people would. How information is collected through the visual, auditory, haptic (touch), olfactory, and proprioceptive (i.e., related to the body's position, orientation in space, and movement) systems can be affected by autism. In any single person, one or more of these sensory channels can be impacted, and a person with autism can be simultaneously hypersensitive to some stimuli and hyposensitive to others. People with autism can also have trouble dealing with and integrating sensory information being received through several different channels at once (e.g., eyes, ears, nose, skin). Autistic people can have compulsive behaviors that have clear design-related ramifications. Differences from one autistic individual to the next make it difficult to generalize about how environmental design can be used to support people with autism.

Experts suggest creating visually and acoustically calming spaces for people with autism.

In general, experts suggest creating visually and acoustically calming spaces for people with autism. These use relaxing colors with low saturation and relatively high brightness, as mentioned in Chapter 2. It is best to minimize patterns in carpets, upholstery, and similar surfaces in places visited by autistic people because autistic individuals can become "stuck" on a particular pattern, repeatedly counting elements, for example. If the autistic person who will use the space you are developing has no history of this sort of behavior and you have reason to believe it will not develop in the future, than feel free to use geometric and similar patterns, although it is important in any case to prevent the visual environment from getting too visually complex. A space with desired levels of visual complexity could have painted walls, single-color carpets, drapes, and upholstery, and only carefully selected photos and decorative items in view. Spaces where autistic individuals can be expected to spend time should also be well ventilated.

Spaces to be used by autistic individuals should not be cluttered; papers and objects should be placed inside cabinets or similar storage units. Some individuals with autism are not aware that they have objects that they can't see, such as clothes, so for those people it is important to find ways to keep objects neatly in view, for example, by providing a shelf on which folded pairs of pants can be piled.

Shadows caused by daylight or uneven lighting can be troubling to people with autism, as can surface shine and resulting glare—but it's important that autistic individuals be exposed to daylight, even indoors. Adding low intensity lighting to eliminate shadows and using matte surfaces instead of smooth, highly polished ones can alleviate many of these issues. So can uplighting, which projects light toward the ceiling and not directly toward the floor. Dimmers can be used to regulate light levels, as can easy to adjust window blinds. Clerestory windows, which are windows so high on a wall that it is generally not possible for someone to see outside through the window, can cut glare; awnings can do so as well. Since people with autism can also be sensitive to bright light, care must be taken not to overlight spaces.

People with autism regularly have difficulty dealing with high-frequency sounds and background noises of the sort created by fans (exhaust and otherwise) as well as air-conditioning and heating systems. Extra quiet heating and air-conditioning systems are therefore generally desirable in homes for people with autism. The sounds of appliances in operation—or the low hum they may make simply because they're plugged in—can be upsetting to some autistic individuals, as can appliances that rock when they operate because they are on an uneven floor. Creaking—in doors or floors—can be problematic. Eliminating these sounds, therefore, from the homes of autistic people to the extent possible seems to be a good idea. Hard surfaces can make it difficult to control noise, so they should be cushioned (with wall hangings and carpeting on floors) when possible.

Autistic people are concerned with maintaining routines, and compartmentalizing spaces can help caregivers do just that. Compartmentalizing means zoning or creating dedicated areas for particular activities, for example, a dressing zone in a bedroom that is distinct from a sleeping space. Compartmentalizing can also limit sensory exposure, which can help people with autism to focus. Ideally, compartmentalized spaces are isolated visually from each other, say with a wall or drape, so that peripheral vision is limited. Acoustic shielding in these areas can also be useful.

Escape zones can also be created for people with autism; the exact form of an escape zone should be based on an individual's hyper- or hypo-sensitivities. So an escape space for someone who is hypersensitive to sound would be soundproofed, while one for someone who is hyposensitive to sound would allow music or other sounds.

Many children with autism wander away from caregivers, so it is important that doors inside their homes and gates in and out of outdoor spaces be secured by whatever means are necessary to prevent individuals from getting lost. With younger children, wandering can be prevented by placing latches in places too high for them to reach, but locks with keys or combinations may be necessary to keep older children from wandering.

The negative behaviors of people with autism are reduced when they are around animals such as pets; they tend to be more social and in better moods. Designing to enhance pets' lives was discussed in Chapter 2.

Autistic individuals are prone to tripping, so it's important that carpets used make it difficult to "catch a toe" and that transitions between rooms be smooth. Area rugs used should be nonslip. To avoid injury, sharp edges on moldings and furniture should be eliminated in spaces that will be used by autistic individuals. Rugs and other resilient surfaces can also prevent some injuries. Stain-resistant materials are also a good idea. It may be necessary to place window blind cords in places where they can't be reached as well as to cover electrical outlets.

Many people with autism are fascinated by the sight of moving water. Spaces for those individuals should not have working faucets and so forth, or operational sources of water should be monitored by a caregiver.

People with autism feel more comfortable entering a room if they can see into it first. Windows in or beside doors and vestibules are therefore desirable when they are feasible.

Mostafa has extensively researched how design can enhance the lives of people with autism, and much of her advice can be implemented in homes. In general, her suggestions involve minimizing sensory stimulation that an autistic person finds troubling and ensuring access to experiences that are comforting for that individual. She has developed an extensive list of recommendations involving design parameters such as ceiling height, visual symmetry and rhythm, texture, ventilation, and room orientation. It is available free of charge at https://archnet.org/publications/5107

Ahrentzen and Steele provide many practical tips for the design of homes where autistic people will be comfortable and safe—they discuss, for example, appropriate water faucet design. Their informative booklet is available without charge at https://bit.ly/2nbchTM

People with Attention Deficit/ Hyperactivity Disorder

A diagnosis of this disorder has design-related ramifications. The design-related experiences of people with Attention Deficit Disorder (ADD) and ADHD are similar enough so that throughout this chapter the same recommendations will be made for people with ADD and ADHD, and people with ADD or ADHD will both be identified as individuals with ADHD.

It is particularly important that the spaces where people with ADHD will need to concentrate, such as places where adults will be doing knowledge work or where children will be studying, be designed to minimize their ADHD related symptoms. Work zones need to be created for adults and children with ADHD. These are places where distractions are minimized and needed tools are readily available. They should be separated from active areas of the home to the extent possible. For example, work zones should if feasible be located away from high traffic areas such as the front door and the family room. They should also be as far as possible from television sets. If televisions can't be removed from an area, they need to be enclosed in armoires or similar pieces of furniture to make them less visible and thus less likely to be turned on when the person with ADHD needs to concentrate. A door that closes helps block out distracting noise from other parts of the home. Some people with ADHD do better with homework and knowledge work when they are in complete silence and others when there is a low murmur of background noise.

Areas where adults or children with ADHD will work should be carefully planned. Relaxing colors should be used on walls and other major surfaces in work zones. As discussed in Chapter 2, relaxing colors are not very saturated but relatively bright—sage green is an example of a relaxing color. Single items such as a stapler or a frame around a bulletin board can be more exciting colors—choose those that are more saturated and less bright, such as pumpkin orange. Research with children with ADHD has shown that they learn best in environments that are moderately stimulating, so it's important that workplaces also be moderately stimulating.

Both adults and children with ADHD also need to work in organized environments, although exactly how those spaces are designed and what is organized will differ by age. Colored folders are one way ADHD folks of all ages can keep track of important paperwork, work to be done, and tasks that are completed. These folders can be stored in file cabinets, cubbyholes on desks, or baskets stored on bookshelves. In any case, all storage spaces should be labeled. Trays should be used to organize supplies, and they can be placed in desk drawers or on shelving units as needed. Tools such as staplers and pens need to be stored near where they will be used. Everything needed must be in the workplace—that avoids distracting trips to retrieve required items.

Colored folders are one way ADHD folks can keep organized.

Organizing systems also can prevent information or objects from being lost, since every time something is lost, it can generate off-task work—objects must be found, the same information gathered again, and so on. The baskets, etc., used to organize materials must be clearly visible, but it's important that the person with ADHD not be able to see the things in these containers after they are stored—if the things remain visible, they remain distracting. In general, workspaces for people with ADHD should have low to moderate visual complexity.

Other tools can help people with ADHD live more "usual" lives. Both adults and children with ADHD benefit from having corkboards and whiteboards where they can write messages to themselves about upcoming events and other dates, or pin materials that require action. Whiteboards, desktop or wall calendars, and clocks can help people with ADHD establish and maintain routines and stay organized; routines help people with ADHD manage their lives more effectively. Having these objects present physically (as opposed to only accessible via an online system) makes them harder to miss. People can't help seeing a corkboard when they enter an office if it is large enough and placed in view; if it is positioned where their eyes will naturally fall, they can't help reviewing the material there, although it is possible to forget or be distracted from accessing an online calendar or system. The important point is to establish a reminder system that is used throughout the area and then use furnishings to support that system.

Task lighting can be used to focus attention, literally, on the job at hand. A desk lamp that lights an area large enough for papers being worked on or materials that need to be read can help people with ADHD stay on task.

Workplaces must be comfortably lit and ventilated to avoid any need to fiddle with lights or thermostats or windows. The workplace should also support the preferred working postures of the person with ADHD—if they like to sit in a club chair with their laptop on their lap and type, they must be able to do so. Alternatively, if the person with ADHD likes to sit on the floor and work with their laptop on a coffee table, a coffee table must be present.

Adults and children with ADHD generally are better able to work and focus after exercise, so either setting up in-home workout space and gear or living in a space near workout facilities, whether formal or informal (i.e., hiking and the like), is a good idea. People with ADHD can also benefit from having sit-stand desks—even more than the rest of the population. Sit-stand desks and their link to well-being were discussed in Chapter 2.

Children with ADHD who have views of nature from their home have fewer symptoms than kids without views of nature. Access to nature views should, therefore, influence the selection of homes where children with ADHD will live and the allocation of bedrooms within those homes.

Inattentive children do better in school when white noise is added to their classrooms, so adding white noise to the home study spaces of people with ADHD can be useful. White noise systems can be sourced online; the volume of the white noise in the classrooms studied was about seventy-five decibels.

People with ADHD can enjoy hands on do-it-yourself and craft type projects, so there must be a space in their home that supports these types of activities. The exact design of the space in question will depend on the specific DIY or craft type activities to be done.

There are a few other considerations for spaces to be used by people with ADHD. Particularly if the ADHD individuals in question are children, breakable objects should be out of reach or otherwise protected. In general, it's important to cushion sharp edges so people with ADHD don't bruise themselves when they move quickly. To minimize having to hunt for stuff, drop-off zones should be created near the main door into the home where keys, phones, and the like can be placed as the person with ADHD returns home. For the same reasons, coatracks and shoe racks are a good idea. Since in general, decorative items are distracting, it's important to keep the general number of knickknacks and pieces of art edited to a relatively low number throughout the home and the environment generally relaxing. Similarly, simple patterns on drapes and carpets are best not only in designated "concentration zones" but throughout the house.

Places in the home where people with ADHD can be expected to work and rest should be designed to be distraction free and generally relatively calming spaces.

For individuals with ADHD, coatracks and shoe racks are a good idea. ───────────

CHAPTER 11

RIGHT PLACE, RIGHT TIME

Designing a home that both uses the environmental psychology research discussed in Chapter 2 and supports the PlaceTypes of the people who live there is a daunting task. The strength of the related scientific work, however, makes it clear that the effort you put into creating an office and home that enhances your well-being will be time well spent. You're likely to feel happier and more satisfied with your office and home as soon as you begin!

But where to begin?

You've already begun. The first and most important steps in the whole process are learning about the basic principles of environmental psychology and determining your PlaceType and those of the people who share your home.

Next, you should take stock of your living situation. What furnishings do you own that must be retained? These are things, perhaps sets of china, a painting, or a sofa, that have been in your family for some time, or to which you or someone else living in your home have a strong sentimental attachment. Make sure that you find a place for these objects in your new home.

When you have done that, inventory the physical condition of your home. What rooms need to be modified to support a PlaceType or to make their design consistent with principles of environmental psychology? Doggedly move through each space in your home. Assess them all.

Your inventory will no doubt indicate a number of steps that you should take to revamp your home. You should begin to modify the design of your home only when you feel confident that the action is justified and that you have the resources—time and money—to be successful at whatever project you begin.

A good first step is to make sure that there is as much sunlight as possible in each room of your house. Natural light has an almost magical effect on people, making them feel good and perform well. Make sure that any modifications you make to add natural light don't create glare. You may need to hang some sheer curtains to add natural light without glare. Also, don't take down so many curtains that your neighbors or people wandering by learn too much about you and your habits. Some things really do need to be kept private. Our species is happiest and healthiest when we sleep in a dark place, so make sure you can darken bedrooms at night.

Once your home is bathed in as much natural light as possible, take whatever steps are required architecturally to align the structure with environmental psychology research and your PlaceType. Carefully weigh expensive decisions, and always work with licensed professionals such as architects. If you can't make changes in your home that seem like a good idea, like opening up walls so there are more windows, work with these professionals to investigate alternatives—for example, skylights and light tubes.

As you're making architectural changes, try to create the places in your home that you'd like to actually use—if you are a potter, you'll want a space to create ceramics; if your partner is a writer, he or she needs a space for writing. Also, heating and lighting zones should line up with the activity zones in your home. In addition, everyone living in your house needs both a territory and a space where they can have privacy—sometimes a place can play both of these roles.

Be particularly careful when planning a home office. A space where you can concentrate and work effectively and efficiently will earn a wonderful return on the resources you commit to creating it.

Next, it's time to work on the interior design of your home, again while considering the sorts of spaces that support your PlaceType. Start with planning floors, because they are the hardest element to change later and often one of the most complex decisions to make. You must reconcile factors such as what a surface looks like with how well it wears and the traffic expected, and whether a type of surface is even a reasonable option where your home is located. Since visible wood grain does such a good job at de-stressing us, hardwood should be a serious consideration for floors throughout your home.

After flooring and rugs are selected, any lighting and sound system issues that remain after architectural modifications are completed at your home will need to be resolved.

Take a look at all of the stuff in your life now—it's unlikely you'll have less in the future. Between built-ins, cabinets, and other storage furniture, you must be able to tuck most of what you own out of sight. There's nothing that makes a human being tense faster than visual clutter.

The larger pieces of furniture needed should be identified before smaller ones are chosen, but none should be purchased until all are selected. Make sure that you have furnishings that make it comfortable for you to be in your home and create comfy spots for guests. Every one of us needs to socialize with other human beings, and all that hanging around together is a lot more pleasant when seats and other furnishings are well designed.

Art and decorative elements, light bulbs, and scents are the final choices you need to make for your home.

Creating a home that supports your psychological well-being is good for you as well as for the planet. If you are happy in your home, you're less likely to feel you need to move, or modify it again in the future, or even build another house, which conserves natural resources. When you apply environmental psychology and support your PlaceType, you'll find that you are happy, health, wealthy (at least in spirit), and wise.

ABOUT THE AUTHOR

Sally Augustin, PhD, is a practicing environmental psychologist and a principal at Design With Science. She has extensive experience integrating science-based insights to develop recommendations for the design of places and objects and provides services that support desired cognitive, emotional, and physical experiences and outcomes. Her clients include individuals, manufacturers, service providers, and design firms worldwide.

Dr. Augustin is a Fellow of the American Psychological Association and holds leadership positions in professional organizations such as the American Psychological Association and the Environmental Design Research Association. She is the author of *Place Advantage: Applied Psychology* for *Interior Architecture* (Wiley, 2009) and, with Cindy Coleman, *The Designer's Guide to Doing Research: Applying Knowledge to Inform Design* (Wiley, 2012). Sally's work has been discussed in publications such as *The New York Times, The Wall Street Journal, The Guardian, Forbes,* and *Psychology Today.* Dr. Augustin is the editor of *Research Design Connections.*

Dr. Augustin has talked about using design to enhance human performance and psychological well-being on mass-market national television and radio programs in the United States and in Europe, as well as on cnn.com and bbc.com. She speaks frequently to audiences in North America, Europe, and Asia at events such as the annual meeting of the American Institute of Architects, the International Design & Emotion Conference, the biannual meeting of the Association of Neuroscience for Architecture, NeoCon/IIDEX, the American Psychological Association's annual meeting, the Environmental Design Research Association annual conference, Living-Futures, and Applied Brilliance. She is a graduate of Wellesley College (BA, economics major), Northwestern University (MBA, majors in finance and marketing), and Claremont Graduate University (PhD, psychology).

To read more from Sally Augustin, please visit https://designwithscience.com/recommended-readings.